END

I am sincerely grateful for the work that Charles Fox has put into his latest project, *Night Vision*. This is a much-needed element for the Body of Christ. Establishing a biblical foundation to understanding dreams and how God can use them is extremely important for our current culture that can easily be swayed by an enemy posing as a good thing, but not a God thing. Through *Night Vision*, Charles has constructed a phenomenal book with real life examples that helps any reader grasp a further understanding, knowledge, and wisdom concerning how God can speak to us through the night. This is a must-have book for anyone who desires to grow in their walk with the Lord!

RYAN JOHNSON
Ryan Johnson Ministries
www.ryanjohnson.us

This is an excellent book on God-given dreams. It is easy to read yet profound. Dr. Fox's work deserves a place in seminary and Bible college courses for its balanced, biblical, practical, and clear focus. I have known Dr. Fox for almost three decades. During all those years he has shown himself to walk in integrity and consistent spiritual perception. His new book on dreams demands serious attention to those interested in the God who communicates.

JON RUTHVEN, PHD
Author, *How Jesus Defined Christianity: His Kingdom/ Spirit Mission and Its 7 Foundational Mandates*

Night Vision is an anointed book with great biblical insight and solid teaching. If you desire to be empowered in understanding and interpreting your dream life and dream language, this message is for you. Revelation and discernment do not sleep! This teaching will give you a strong biblical foundation, spiritual depth, insight, accuracy, and maturity on how to know and advance in the messages the Lord is releasing in the night hours through night visions and dreams. I greatly appreciate this manuscript that Dr. Charles Fox has scribed. It is written from personal supernatural encounters and experiences that carry life, revelation, and wisdom from heaven. Thank you, Charles, for this anointed training, empowering, and activating message!

REBECCA GREENWOOD
Cofounder of Christian Harvest International
Strategic Prayer Apostolic Network
Author of *Glory Warfare* and *Discerning the Spirit Realm*

My dear friend Dr. Charles Fox's new book *Night Vision* will not only help you understand your dreams, but will help you grow in your relationship with the Lord. I so appreciate the biblical scholarship and the amazing stories in this book, and so will you. Much of my ministry can be directed back to God directing my life through dreams, and I wish this book had been available to me 30 years ago. Beloved, commit yourself to prayer and the scriptures, read this book, and get ready for your personal dream journey with God.

WILL FORD
Founder of Dreamstreamco.com and 818thesign.org
Author of *The Dream King: How the Dream of Martin Luther King Jr. Is Being Fulfilled To Heal Racism in America*

Throughout Scripture, we see God speaking to His people through dreams and visions. The God we encounter in the Bible is still very much at work in our lives and world today, and He longs to communicate with us in that same way. Charles Fox's new book *Night Vision* will help you grow in your journey of dreaming with God and give you the tools to unpack and understand what He's saying to you at night.

SHAUN TABATT
Publishing Executive, Destiny Image

NIGHT VISION

MAKING SENSE OF
SUPERNATURAL DREAM ENCOUNTERS

CHARLES R. FOX

DESTINY IMAGE® PUBLISHERS, INC.

P.O. Box 310, Shippensburg, PA 17257-0310

"Promoting Inspired Lives."

This book and all other Destiny Image and Destiny Image Fiction books are available at Christian bookstores and distributors worldwide.

For more information on foreign distributors, call 717-532-3040.

Reach us on the Internet: www.destinyimage.com.

ISBN 13 TP: 978-0-7684-6220-3
ISBN 13 eBook: 978-0-7684-6221-0

For Worldwide Distribution, Printed in the U.S.A.

1 2 3 4 5 6 7 8 / 26 25 24 23 22

DEDICATION

I want to first give thanks to my Lord and Savior Jesus Christ. None of this would be possible without Him giving me the strength. I dedicate this book to my loving wife April, our children—Gabby and Isaiah—and the late John Paul Jackson. Even though we never officially met, you were my mentor and teacher from afar. I also want to thank the following people: my dad, Charles R. Fox, Sr. (thank you, Dad, for leading me to the Lord and being such a great man of faith); my mom, Vicky Fox (Mombo) Mccallister (thanks for your love and always believing in me); my friend, Jon Ruthven (I love you, "Doc"); and finally Randy Clark (thank you for writing the foreword to this book). It is truly an honor to co-labor with you in this new season!

CONTENTS

FOREWORD

Charles Fox's new book, *Night Vision: Making Sense of Supernatural Dream Encounters,* is an informative study regarding spiritual dreams. Dr. Fox from Regent University in Renewal Studies provides biblical insights regarding dreams. Examples of dreams from both the Old Testament and New Testament are provided. He points out how the Bible provides discernment between dreams that are from God, from demonic sources, or from the human spirit resulting often from unresolved issues, conflicts, and concerns. He provides an entire chapter to deal with counterfeit or deceptive dreams. In this chapter he also deals with dark/discouraging dreams and how to handle them. Dr. Fox provides insight in how to interpret the many different symbols in our dreams.

Dr. Fox presents twenty-one dreams that were significant in his life. He emphasizes the importance of the context of dreams, which he provides, the dream itself, and then the interpretation of the dream and the significance it had upon his life. This was a learning experience for me. His stories of how God led him in making decisions and kept him from making mistakes through his dreams were encouraging.

It was an interesting read that was not overly academic but much more a personal self-disclosure of Dr. Fox's learning curve. Especially intriguing to me was how God used prophecy and dreams to lead him to his wife and to break up with his girlfriend before he met his wife. Dreams that helped him with his children, warning about problems in his church that would have happened if he hadn't been warned not to appoint someone to key leadership, about revival, about drugs, a warning about a famous pastor who was morally compromised and doctrinally unorthodox and to stay his distance from the pastor, dreams pointing to directions regarding spiritual warfare, positive dreams, dreams indicating the importance of obedience, a comforting dream for his most painful experience in life, dreams that let him know about a student who was in financial need, a dream that would give Dr. Fox more faith for defeating the demonic attacks upon his life, and a dream that would encourage him regarding the baptism in the Holy Spirit.

There was a chapter that dealt with how to be more receptive to spiritual dreams from God. In this chapter Dr. Fox shares seven things we can do to increase the dream activity in our lives and our ability to better discern their source and interpret them.

Dr. Fox ends the book with a prayer for the reader for a greater activation related to spiritual dreams and an impartation to have more spiritual dreams.

Night Vision is an informative, interesting, easy to read, most practical guide for anyone wanting to grow in having and interpreting spiritual dreams. I recommend it. I also recommend Dr. Fox who is one of our professors at Global Awakening Theological Seminary. He is a man who loves people and God and who wants to serve God by serving God's people.

RANDY CLARK, Revivalist
Overseer of the Apostolic Network of Global Awakening
President of Global Awakening
President of Global Awakening Theological Seminary
Author of *Intimacy with God* and 40 other books

INTRODUCTION

Recently there have been several books on the subject of dreams, visions, and how to operate in the seer realm, or spiritual sight realm. As a person who has been dreaming since I was a young boy living in Brooklyn, New York, I felt led by the Holy Spirit to write a book about dreams that approaches the subject from a lifelong dreamer's perspective.

After reading several dream manuscripts and listening to people, I became convinced that there needed to be a book written that focuses solely on actual dreams with their interpretations.

Though there is good material on dreams, many readers want more examples of dreams along with their actual interpretation so they can learn the way God speaks in dreams and how to interpret their own dreams.

This book, *Night Vision: Making Sense of Supernatural Dream Encounters,* does just that for them—and you.

Although the first chapter of the book sets the biblical basis and foundation by giving select examples from the Old and New Testaments regarding the importance of dreams, the majority of the remaining chapters draw from my personal journey in supernatural dream encounters.

Similar to the parables our Lord Jesus used to teach His disciples and the multitudes about the Kingdom of God, by the grace of God, I retell my dream encounters along with the interpretations. It is my prayer that after you are finished reading this book, you will receive an impartation to see into the spirit realm through dreams, to learn how to interpret your own dreams, and to help others understand their dreams for the purpose of drawing closer to the Lord.

1

THE BIBLICAL FRAMEWORK FOR DREAMS

For God may speak in one way, or in another, yet man does not perceive it. In a dream, in a vision of the night, when deep sleep falls upon men, while slumbering on their beds, then He opens the ears of men, and seals their instruction (Job 33:14-16 NKJV).

Many people today have a fascination with dreams. Just do a search about interpreting your dreams on the Internet and look at how many references actually come up. You will get topics ranging from psychological interpretations to the psychic or spiritual meanings behind dreams.

The purpose of this chapter, however, is to provide a biblical framework for dreams and their interpretations by highlighting select examples from the Old and New Testaments.

OLD TESTAMENT EXAMPLES

Abimelech

The first dream mentioned in the Bible actually concerns Abraham and his wife Sarah. Due to Sarah's beauty even as an older woman, Abraham was willing to risk the possibility of another man sleeping with his wife when he told Abimelech, king of Gerar, that Sarah was just his sister. He had already used this tactic successfully in his interaction with Pharaoh when he traveled to Egypt because of a famine (see Genesis 12:10-20). The story follows:

> *Abraham journeyed from there to the South, and dwelt between Kadesh and Shur, and stayed in Gerar. Now Abraham said of Sarah his wife, "She is my sister." And Abimelech king of Gerar sent and took Sarah. But God came to Abimelech in a dream by night, and said to him, "Indeed you are a dead man because of the*

woman whom you have taken, for she is a man's wife." But Abimelech had not come near her; and he said, "Lord, will You slay a righteous nation also? Did he not say to me, 'She is my sister'? And she, even she herself said, 'He is my brother.' In the integrity of my heart and innocence of my hands I have done this."

And God said to him in a dream, "Yes, I know that you did this in the integrity of your heart. For I also withheld you from sinning against Me; therefore I did not let you touch her. Now therefore, restore the man's wife; for he is a prophet, and he will pray for you and you shall live. But if you do not restore her, know that you shall surely die, you and all who are yours" (Genesis 20:1-7 NKJV).

I love this story because it reveals the grace of God in the midst of human weakness and imperfection. Though Abraham would be called the father of our faith, his own faith had to mature. Even though God had appeared to him several times and had promised protection in Genesis 15:1 (NIV), *"I am your shield,"* provision in Genesis 17:1 (NKJV), *"I am Almighty God,"* and a legacy in Genesis 12:2-3 (NKJV), *"I will make you a great nation,"* the former "moon worshipper" from Ur still struggled with trusting the Lord at times.

How many times have we behaved just like Abraham? Sometimes we struggle with doubts and oftentimes try to fix situations ourselves, but God always proves Himself faithful. Similar to Abraham, the Lord does not stop working behind the scenes in our lives because of our lack of faith in various situations. Our faith is strengthened through every test we pass and in the ones we fail. Dreams are a way God speaks to us and builds our faith.

The Lord was moving the needle of Abraham's faith from doubt to radical trust with every test. Knowing God rescued Sarah behind the scenes through Abimelech's dream grew Abraham's faith and prepared him to pass the greatest test of his life.

In the same way we trust Jesus to be our sacrifice, Abraham trusted God to provide a sacrifice:

> *Now it came to pass after these things that God tested Abraham, and said to him, "Abraham!"*
> *And he said, "Here I am."*
> *Then He said, "Take now your son, your only son Isaac, whom you love, and go to the land of Moriah, and offer him there as a burnt offering on one of the mountains of which I shall tell you."*
> *So Abraham rose early in the morning and saddled his donkey, and took two of his young*

*men with him, and Isaac his son; and he split
the wood for the burnt offering, and arose and
went to the place of which God had told him.
Then on the third day Abraham lifted his eyes
and saw the place afar off. And Abraham said to
his young men, "Stay here with the donkey; the
lad and I will go yonder and worship, and we
will come back to you."*

*So Abraham took the wood of the burnt offering
and laid it on Isaac his son; and he took the fire
in his hand, and a knife, and the two of them
went together. But Isaac spoke to Abraham his
father and said, "My father!"*

And he said, "Here I am, my son."

*Then he said, "Look, the fire and the wood, but
where is the lamb for a burnt offering?"*

*And Abraham said, "My son, God will provide
for Himself the lamb for a burnt offering." So
the two of them went together* (Genesis 22:1-8
NKJV).

Abraham's faith had now grown from a man who
would shrink back in fear to a man who had such strong
faith that he was not only willing to sacrifice his son,
but trusted God to actually raise Isaac from the dead,

a foreshadowing of how God would sacrifice His Son, Jesus, and raise Him from the dead.

> *It was by faith that Abraham offered Isaac as a sacrifice when God was testing him. Abraham, who had received God's promises, was ready to sacrifice his only son, Isaac, even though God had told him, "Isaac is the son through whom your descendants will be counted." Abraham reasoned that if Isaac died, God was able to bring him back to life again. And in a sense, Abraham did receive his son back from the dead* (Hebrews 11:17-19 NLT).

Although there were certainly other miraculous events that grew Abraham's faith to the point of sacrificing his son—the birth of Isaac in his old age, financial blessing, divine protection, etc.— the dream that God gave Abimelech to protect Sarah was an important foundational piece in Abraham's faith walk.

Jacob

Abraham's grandson, Jacob, is another important figure in the Old Testament, especially as it pertains to dreams. Jacob, the second born of Isaac's sons, had to flee his father's house for his life to avoid the wrath of his brother Esau after stealing his birthright (see Genesis 27:41-45). As Jacob journeyed toward his uncle Laban's house to Padan Aram, he had an important dream encounter with the Lord that transformed his life.

> *Now Jacob went out from Beersheba and went toward Haran. So he came to a certain place and stayed there all night, because the sun had set. And he took one of the stones of that place and put it at his head, and he lay down in that place to sleep. Then he dreamed, and behold, a ladder was set up on the earth, and its top reached to heaven; and there the angels of God were ascending and descending on it.*
>
> *And behold, the Lord stood above it and said: "I am the Lord God of Abraham your father and the God of Isaac; the land on which you lie I will give to you and your descendants. Also your descendants shall be as the dust of the earth; you shall spread abroad to the west and the east, to the north and the south; and in you and in your seed all the families of the earth shall be blessed. Behold, I am with you and will keep you wherever you go, and will bring you back to this land; for I will not leave you until I have done what I have spoken to you."*
>
> *Then Jacob awoke from his sleep and said, "Surely the Lord is in this place, and I did not*

know it." And he was afraid and said, "How awesome is this place! This is none other than the house of God, and this is the gate of heaven!" (Genesis 28:10-17 NKJV)

This particular prophetic dream that God gave Jacob was a great source of encouragement to him. Through the dream, the Lord confirmed His promises: that He was with Jacob and would protect Jacob wherever he went; He would bring him back to Luz, later Bethel; and never leave him until these promises were kept. Prophetic dreams accomplish the same purposes that verbal prophecies accomplish. They help edify, encourage, warn, give direction, and alert us of events to come. Jacob needed to be reminded that God would be with him on his journey and he would be protected.

In the chapters that follow, I discuss prophetic dreams in more detail and explain how important they have been in my life.

As previously mentioned, the Lord gave Jacob a dream as he began his journey to a new place, the house of Laban. God also gave Jacob a second important dream when it was time for him to return home from Laban's house after he had stayed with his uncle for twenty years. During that time, he acquired two wives and many children. Unfortunately for Jacob, he had met his match in Laban, who was more of a deceiver than he himself was.

First, Laban had promised Jacob his daughter Rachel in marriage, but on Jacob's wedding night, Laban tricked Jacob into sleeping with his older daughter, Leah (see Genesis 29:18-25). After fulfilling seven days of the marriage feast, Laban gave Jacob Rachel as his second wife for a price of seven more years of labor.

After the seven years of working for Rachel, the Lord gave Jacob a divine directive to leave the service of his uncle. In addition to Laban tricking Jacob to work for him longer, his uncle also cheated Jacob by changing his wages ten times during his tenure as a shepherd (Genesis 31:7).

Then the Lord spoke to Jacob through another dream. Through this dream, God gave Jacob insight to how to multiply his flock to provide for his family and also direction about returning to the land of his birth.

> *One time during the mating season, I had a dream and saw that the male goats mating with the females were streaked, speckled, and spotted. Then in my dream, the angel of God said to me, "Jacob!" And I replied, "Yes, here I am."*
>
> *The angel said, "Look up, and you will see that only the streaked, speckled, and spotted males are mating with the females of your flock. For I have seen how Laban has treated you. I am*

the God who appeared to you at Bethel, the place where you anointed the pillar of stone and made your vow to me. Now get ready and leave this country and return to the land of your birth" (Genesis 31:10-13 NLT).

Though Bible scholars are divided as to whether or not God revealed to Jacob a step-by-step exit strategy for blessing and for departing the service of a con man, it is clear from the story in Genesis 31 that God gave Jacob direction and confirmation. It was time to *"get ready and leave this country and return to the land of your birth."* To fully understand the story and grasp the impact of the dream, we must first review the agreement that Jacob made with Laban earlier in the narrative.

In Genesis 30:25-28 (NLT), Jacob tells Laban he wants to leave with his family and reminds Laban that he worked hard for him and earned his independence. Laban admits right up front that it is because of Jacob's hard work and favor that he has become wealthy. Laban says he will pay whatever Jacob says.

Soon after Rachel had given birth to Joseph, Jacob said to Laban, "Please release me so I can go home to my own country. Let me take my wives and children, for I have earned them by serving you, and let me be on my way. You certainly know how hard I have worked for you."

"Please listen to me," Laban replied. "I have become wealthy, for the Lord has blessed me because of you. Tell me how much I owe you. Whatever it is, I'll pay it."

In verses 29-33, Jacob repeats his request and reminder that he is the reason behind Jacob's wealth. But this time, when Laban asks what Jacob wants, Jacob strikes up a deal. He doesn't want wages—he wants all Laban's speckled, spotted, and black sheep and Jacob will continue to watch Laban's flocks.

Jacob replied, "You know how hard I've worked for you, and how your flocks and herds have grown under my care. You had little indeed before I came, but your wealth has increased enormously. The Lord has blessed you through everything I've done. But now, what about me? When can I start providing for my own family?"

"What wages do you want?" Laban asked again.

Jacob replied, "Don't give me anything. Just do this one thing, and I'll continue to tend and watch over your flocks. Let me inspect your flocks today and remove all the sheep and goats that are speckled or spotted, along with all the black sheep. Give these to me as my wages. In the future, when you check on the animals you have given me as my wages, you'll see that I have been honest. If you find in my flock any goats without speckles or spots, or any sheep that are not black, you will know that I have stolen them from you."

In verses 34-40, Laban agrees to Jacob's request but then double-crosses him and hides all the blemished sheep with his sons a good distance away. However, because Jacob was given supernatural insight by an angel through a dream (Genesis 31:10), he can build his own flock instead of increasing Laban's.

"All right," Laban replied. "It will be as you say." But that very day Laban went out and removed the male goats that were streaked and spotted, all the female goats that were speckled and spotted or had white patches, and all the black sheep. He placed them in the care of his own sons, who took them a three-days' journey from where Jacob was. Meanwhile, Jacob stayed and cared for the rest of Laban's flock.

Then Jacob took some fresh branches from poplar, almond, and plane trees and peeled off strips of bark, making white streaks on them. Then he placed these peeled branches in the

watering troughs where the flocks came to drink,
for that was where they mated. And when they
mated in front of the white-streaked branches,
they gave birth to young that were streaked,
speckled, and spotted. Jacob separated those
lambs from Laban's flock. And at mating time
he turned the flock to face Laban's animals that
were streaked or black. This is how he built his
own flock instead of increasing Laban's (Genesis
30:34-40 NLT).

After studying this passage, I am convinced there are two ways to look at this story.

The first view basically centers on one con man losing to another, but God in His sovereignty still uses Jacob's imperfections to fulfill His overall plan. In essence, this position asserts that God gave Jacob a second dream simply to confirm the timing of his exit from Laban and to affirm Jacob's odd breeding program, which the Lord sovereignly backed to bless Jacob.

The second view, however, suggests that God was the One who planted the idea to breed the animals in Jacob's mind through the dream by showing him that only the streaked, speckled, or spotted males should breed with the females. God is sovereign! By way of a dream, God blessed the plan He had given to Jacob and made him wealthy before he departed from his dishonest uncle.

The Lord's sovereign protection was again on display after Jacob sneaked away with his wives, children, and animals. Laban furiously pursued Jacob with the intent to harm him, but God halted Laban with a dream that warned him to reconsider.

> *And Laban was told on the third day that Jacob had fled. Then he took his brethren with him and pursued him for seven days' journey, and he overtook him in the mountains of Gilead. But God had come to Laban the Syrian in a dream by night, and said to him, "Be careful that you speak to Jacob neither good nor bad"* (Genesis 31:22-24 NKJV).

Whatever view you ascribe to regarding Jacob's breeding program, it is clear that through Jacob's dream about the flocks, God gave him direction and in it demonstrated His perfect timing. Furthermore, God protected Jacob from Laban's wrath by warning Laban in a dream not to interfere with His perfect plan for Jacob. Jacob's and Laban's dream encounters should encourage us that we serve a mighty God who will speak to us through dreams that guide our steps, direct our actions, and protect us.

Joseph

Possibly the most talked about example of God encounters through dreams in the Old Testament is in the life of Joseph. Joseph, the firstborn son of Jacob and his favorite wife Rachel, was a gifted young man. Jacob showed favoritism by giving Joseph a coat of many colors, which contributed to the jealousy of his siblings. To add insult to injury, God began to give Joseph dreams about his future greatness, which Joseph shared with his brothers, making them even more resentful of him.

> *"...Please hear this dream which I have dreamed: There we were, binding sheaves in the field. Then behold, my sheaf arose and also stood upright; and indeed your sheaves stood all around and bowed down to my sheaf."*
>
> *And his brothers said to him, "Shall you indeed reign over us? Or shall you indeed have dominion over us?" So they hated him even more for his dreams and for his words.*
>
> *Then he dreamed still another dream and told it to his brothers, and said, "Look, I have dreamed another dream. And this time, the sun, the moon, and the eleven stars bowed down to me"* (Genesis 37:6-9 NKJV).

Though Joseph's prophetic dream came to pass when he was promoted to second in command in Egypt under Pharaoh, we learn an important lesson from Joseph about sharing our dreams with the wrong people. His brothers became so impassioned with rage that they threw him in a pit and sold him into slavery (see Genesis 37:5-10; 37:18-36; 41:37-45). We must use wisdom in sharing our dreams. I address this important aspect a bit later in the book.

Dreams of the Butler and the Baker

Joseph was not just a dreamer, he was also an *interpreter* of dreams. While in Egypt, Joseph became the slave of Potiphar, who was an officer of the Pharaoh. The Lord was with Joseph and he quickly gained favor with Potiphar, becoming the overseer of the Egyptian captain's entire house (Genesis 39:2-6).

Due to Joseph's handsome appearance, Potiphar's wife began to look at him lustfully. She became relentless in her pursuit of Joseph, demanding that he sleep with her. Although Joseph continually refused her advances, one day she grabbed him by his garment and demanded again that he sleep with her. When Joseph refused again by running away, his cloak was still in the hands of Potiphar's wife. She accused Joseph of raping her, while holding the "said evidence" before the authorities.

Though Joseph was thrown in prison for falsely being accused of the crime of rape, God still was with him and was sovereignly working behind the scenes on his behalf. Having gained favor with the warden of the prison, Joseph was assigned to serve two officials of the court of Pharaoh who lost favor and were also thrown in prison—the cupbearer and the baker.

One morning as Joseph came to serve the two officials, the countenance of both men had changed to sadness. Both men were troubled over the dreams they had the night before.

> *Then the chief butler told his dream to Joseph, and said to him, "Behold, in my dream a vine was before me, and in the vine were three branches; it was as though it budded, its blossoms shot forth, and its clusters brought forth ripe grapes. Then Pharaoh's cup was in my hand; and I took the grapes and pressed them into Pharaoh's cup, and placed the cup in Pharaoh's hand."*
>
> *And Joseph said to him, "This is the interpretation of it: The three branches are three days. Now within three days Pharaoh will lift up your head and restore you to your place, and you will put Pharaoh's cup in his hand according to the*

former manner, when you were his butler. But remember me when it is well with you, and please show kindness to me; make mention of me to Pharaoh, and get me out of this house. For indeed I was stolen away from the land of the Hebrews; and also I have done nothing here that they should put me into the dungeon."

When the chief baker saw that the interpretation was good, he said to Joseph, "I also was in my dream, and there were three white baskets on my head. In the uppermost basket were all kinds of baked goods for Pharaoh, and the birds ate them out of the basket on my head."

So Joseph answered and said, "This is the interpretation of it: The three baskets are three days. Within three days Pharaoh will lift off your head from you and hang you on a tree; and the birds will eat your flesh from you" (Genesis 40:9-19 NKJV).

As we evaluate the dreams and interpretation of these two officials from Pharaoh's court, we see that they both had prophetic dreams. Notice that Joseph draws their attention to the three branches.

Numbers in dreams are extremely important and should be studied. In the cupbearer's case the three branches represented three days into the future when his sentence would be completed and he would be released from prison and restored to his position. The number three was also in the dream of the baker but unfortunately for him, his life would be *completed* (ended) in three days because Pharaoh planned to hang him. Regardless, three is a sign of completion or something coming full circle.

Also, it is important to point out that in Joseph's interpretation of the baker's prophetic dream, birds eating the bread from trays shows the supernatural at work in Joseph's explanation. Remember that the Holy Spirit is the One who gives us the wisdom to understand what symbols mean in dreams depending on the context. There are times when birds in dreams can be a good sign. For example, a dove represents the Holy Spirit bringing peace, and an eagle soaring high above the clouds represents God's strength, protection, and rod of discipline. (See Matthew 3:16; Luke 3:22; Exodus 19:4; Isaiah 40:3; Jeremiah 4:13.)

On the other hand, birds eating from the baskets on the head of the baker was a devastatingly negative sign of impending doom for the baker because the food that he prepared was not being eaten by Pharaoh but by the scavengers of the air. Joseph picked up on this symbolism for two reasons. One reason was *supernatural* in that

God gifted him to understand dreams (Genesis 40:8). But it was also *natural* because Joseph had been living in Egypt, he would naturally know that carnivorous birds were sacred. They swarmed in great numbers because it was unlawful to destroy them. Though God is ultimately the One who gives the interpretation of spiritual dreams, the human element also plays a part in deciphering the meaning. Let me explain with a Scripture verse from Proverbs:

> *It is the glory of God to conceal a matter, but the glory of kings is to search out a matter* (Proverbs 25:2 NKJV).

This verse in Proverbs 25 is important because it gives us insight in the way we are to approach dreams. The Lord will mask the truth in dreams because He wants *us* to search out the clues that He leaves for us. Oftentimes people get frustrated with their dreams because they don't carefully search out the meaning for themselves and have become a bit lazy.

I heard Bethel Church leader Bill Johnson say that "God is not hiding truth *from* you, He is hiding it *for* you." If we are to truly understand our dreams, we must realize a dichotomy is always at work when we are given dreams by Heaven—the human and the divine. God wants us to first cooperate with Him by asking Him for wisdom, by seeking advice from trusted counselors, and by doing some research if necessary or by just being an observer of nature as in the case of Joseph.

Pharaoh's Dreams

Though Joseph had correctly interpreted the dreams of the cupbearer and the baker and asked the cupbearer to remember him when he was freed from prison, Joseph stayed incarcerated for another two years. Little did Joseph know that God was still working behind the scenes— Pharaoh himself began to have dreams.

> *Then it came to pass, at the end of two full years, that Pharaoh had a dream; and behold, he stood by the river. Suddenly there came up out of the river seven cows, fine looking and fat; and they fed in the meadow. Then behold, seven other cows came up after them out of the river, ugly and gaunt, and stood by the other cows on the bank of the river. And the ugly and gaunt cows ate up the seven fine looking and fat cows. So Pharaoh awoke. He slept and dreamed a second time; and suddenly seven heads of grain came up on one stalk, plump and good. Then behold, seven thin heads, blighted by the east wind, sprang up after them. And the seven*

thin heads devoured the seven plump and full heads... (Genesis 41:1-7 NKJV).

Again the sovereignty of God would be on full display in the story of Joseph when the cupbearer, having witnessed Joseph's ability to interpret dreams, told Pharaoh about the Hebrew servant who had accurately predicted his release from prison as well as the demise of his colleague, the baker. The stage was now set for Joseph's gift to make "room for him" and bring him before the king (Proverbs 18:16).

We can profit with a few lessons from Joseph's interaction with Pharaoh.

> *Then Pharaoh sent and called Joseph, and they brought him quickly out of the dungeon; and he shaved, changed his clothing, and came to Pharaoh. And Pharaoh said to Joseph, "I have had a dream, and there is no one who can interpret it. But I have heard it said of you that you can understand a dream, to interpret it." So Joseph answered Pharaoh, saying, "It is not in me; God will give Pharaoh an answer of peace"* (Genesis 41:14-16 NKJV).

First, notice Joseph's humility when Pharaoh compliments Joseph about what he heard from the cupbearer about his ability to interpret dreams. Joseph simply tells Pharaoh that *"It is not in me"* to interpret. Joseph gives all of the glory to God and reassures Pharaoh that God will give the Egyptian leader an answer of peace.

Joseph could have taken this opportunity to impress Pharaoh, especially considering his present circumstances. Joseph chose, however, to make known *his God* to Pharaoh. He wanted the Egyptian leader to know that God was his Source and the One who would explain his dreams. What happened next would change Joseph's life forever as he accurately interpreted Pharaoh's dreams and was promoted to second in command in Egypt (Genesis 41:25-45).

TRANSFORMING IMPACT OF DREAMS AND VISIONS

I believe the Lord Jesus is raising up leaders like Joseph who will serve in every sphere of society, especially politics. The Holy Spirit will give them insight by visiting them with dreams and also give them wisdom to interpret the dreams of others. Like Joseph, these leaders will walk in integrity and not compromise. They will pray in the Holy Spirit and the Lord will show them the future. In the same way, it was by the Holy Spirit that Peter made an important statement on the day of Pentecost about the role that dreams and visions would play in the end-time harvest when quoting the prophet Joel:

But Peter, standing up with the eleven, raised his voice and said to them, "Men of Judea and all who dwell in Jerusalem, let this be known to you, and heed my words. For these are not drunk, as you suppose, since it is only the third hour of the day. But this is what was spoken by the prophet Joel: 'And it shall come to pass in the last days, says God, that I will pour out of My Spirit on all flesh; your sons and your daughters shall prophesy, your young men shall see visions, your old men shall dream dreams'" (Acts 2:14-17 NKJV).

Two words stand out in Peter's declaration: visions and dreams. The Greek word for *vision* in the passage from Acts 2:14-17 is ὅρασις *hŏrasis,* which comes from root word ὅραμα *hŏrama* and denotes an inspired appearance, sight, or vision. The closer we get to the return of the Lord, visions will increase and become a normal occurrence for believers. Even now, as of this writing, I have heard many reports of believers having visions while attending Christian conferences.

Visions have the ability to shift the trajectory of our lives and transform the collective life of the Body of Christ as a whole. The apostle Peter is a great example of this truth.

The next day, as they went on their journey and drew near the city, Peter went up on the housetop to pray, about the sixth hour. Then he became very hungry and wanted to eat; but while they made ready, he fell into a trance and saw heaven opened and an object like a great sheet bound at the four corners, descending to him and let down to the earth. In it were all kinds of four-footed animals of the earth, wild beasts, creeping things, and birds of the air. And a voice came to him, "Rise, Peter; kill and eat." But Peter said, "Not so, Lord! For I have never eaten anything common or unclean." And a voice spoke to him again the second time, "What God has cleansed you must not call common." This was done three times. And the object was taken up into heaven again (Acts 10:9-16 NKJV).

I love this story in the book of Acts because it demonstrates how one supernatural encounter with the Lord can shift the entire mindset of the Church. Up until that time, the fledgling New Testament Church was Jewish. Although there were several Gentiles who encountered Jesus and believed His message during His time on the earth, His primary ministry was to the Jews (see Matthew 15:24). Peter and the rest of the apostles had the mindset of many Jews about being separate from Gentiles. Even after his vision in Acts, Paul still had to confront Peter's hypocrisy concerning the Gentiles in Galatia.

> *When Peter visited Antioch, he caused the believers to stumble over his behavior, so I confronted him to his face. He enjoyed eating with the gentile believers who didn't keep the Jewish customs—up until the time Jacob's Jewish friends arrived from Jerusalem. When he saw them, he withdrew from his gentile friends— fearing how it would look to them if he ate with gentile believers.*
>
> *And so, because of Peter's hypocrisy, many other Jewish believers followed suit, refusing to eat with gentile believers. Even Barnabas was led astray by their hypocritical behavior!*
>
> *So when I realized they were acting inconsistently with the revelation of the gospel, I confronted Peter in front of everyone: "You were born a Jew, but you've chosen to disregard Jewish regulations and live like a gentile. Why then do you force gentiles to conform to these same rules?"* (Galatians 2:11-14 TPT)

As we observe the way Peter shunned the Gentile believers in the presence of his Jewish brothers, we see how important it was for him to have the earlier vision. Because the Jews were no longer under the law, the animals were not considered unclean. In the same way, the Gentiles were cleansed and the Jews did not have to separate from them. Paul, quite rightly, referred to Peter as acting hypocritically: Peter was corrected for preaching grace but living under the law.

Any time we encounter God through dreams or visions, it is because He wants to impact our lives in such a way we will never be the same. Even though Peter caved to the demands of the Judaizers, he accepted Paul's rebuke and gave respect to Paul as an apostle in his later epistles. Peter was more prepared to receive correction from Paul due to his vision about the four-footed animals and other unclean creatures (Acts 10:12).

Like visions, dreams have the same ability to transform our lives. In the last chapter of Acts, Peter again quoted the prophet Joel: *"Your young men shall see visions, your old men shall dream dreams"* (Acts 2:17 NKJV). The word for dreams in the Greek here is *ĕnupniazŏmai* from the root word *ĕnupniŏn*. Explicitly, a dream is a vision as we are in sleep mode. We should never underestimate the power of a dream. Through them we are able to receive instruction, direction, warnings about future events, encouragement, etc. In essence, God can give you a dream that can reshape your destiny.

Before looking at some New Testament dream stories, let's examine one more example from the Old Testament and how this person's life was transformed by dreams.

Nebuchadnezzar

Nebuchadnezzar, the king of Babylon, was an important figure in the Old Testament. He was used by God as an instrument to judge Israel for their blatant idolatry. It was common for ancient kings like Nebuchadnezzar to bring young men like Daniel, who was among the exiles from Israel, to serve in the royal palace. The Babylonian leader was not ready, however, for what God was about to show him through a dream about his kingdom.

> *Now in the second year of Nebuchadnezzar's reign, Nebuchadnezzar had dreams; and his spirit was so troubled that his sleep left him. Then the king gave the command to call the magicians, the astrologers, the sorcerers, and the Chaldeans to tell the king his dreams. So they came and stood before the king. And the king said to them, "I have had a dream, and my spirit is anxious to know the dream."*

Then the Chaldeans spoke to the king in Aramaic, "O king, live forever! Tell your servants the dream, and we will give the interpretation." The king answered and said to the Chaldeans, "My decision is firm: if you do not make known the dream to me, and its interpretation, you shall be cut in pieces, and your houses shall be made an ash heap. However, if you tell the dream and its interpretation, you shall receive from me gifts, rewards, and great honor. Therefore tell me the dream and its interpretation" (Daniel 2:1-6 NKJV).

The king's request for his cadre of magicians, sorcerers, and astrologers to tell him his dream without prior knowledge of it and then interpret it was a tall order. Their response to the king's request was one of disbelief and great consternation. Nebuchadnezzar became incensed when his wise men claimed that no one could do what he was asking of them (Daniel 2:10-11). Unfortunately for the wise men, Nebuchadnezzar became enraged and started killing them (Daniel 2:12-13).

Daniel, also considered among the nucleus of wise men in Babylon, was also in danger. It was at this time that Daniel approached the king.

When Arioch, the commander of the king's guard, came to kill them, Daniel handled the situation with wisdom and discretion. He asked Arioch, "Why has the king issued such a harsh decree?" So Arioch told him all that had happened. Daniel went at once to see the king and requested more time to tell the king what the dream meant.

Then Daniel went home and told his friends Hananiah, Mishael, and Azariah what had happened. He urged them to ask the God of heaven to show them his mercy by telling them the secret, so they would not be executed along with the other wise men of Babylon. That night the secret was revealed to Daniel in a vision. Then Daniel praised the God of heaven (Daniel 2:14-19 NLT).

Imagine if believers today were put in this dire predicament like Daniel and his friends, where their lives hung in the balance of their interpretation of a dream! Everyone would show up for prayer service.

I love how Daniel responded to the crisis. Daniel inquired of the Lord but also enlisted prayer support from Hananiah, Mishael, and Azariah (also known as Shadrach, Meshach, and Abednego). Daniel teaches us an important lesson about dream interpretation in this context. We should always approach the subject of dreams with much prayer, keeping in mind that the Source of revelation for spiritual dreams is God Almighty. As believers, approaching the Lord about our dreams seems like an obvious thing to do. This has not been my experience, however, when interviewing people about their dreams. Although most people desire to understand their dreams, they have not spent time praying over them or asking others to actually pray for the interpretation.

Consider Daniel 2:26-30 (NKJV). Daniel's situation was unique. Nebuchadnezzar not only gave Daniel the dream to interpret, but Daniel had to reveal the dream itself. In essence, he was proving the legitimacy of the Hebrew God who knew and would supernaturally reveal the dream to Daniel. Unlike the other magicians and astrologers and soothsayers, Daniel knew the dream because he knew and trusted *"the God of heaven who reveals secrets."* Moreover, the secret was revealed to Daniel not because he was wiser than the others, but for the "sakes" of the others (verse 30). Basically, so Nebuchadnezzar would not kill them like he had the last group. God had heard their cry for mercy and answered their prayers.

The king answered and said to Daniel, whose name was Belteshazzar, "Are you able to make known to me the dream which I have seen, and its interpretation?"

Daniel answered in the presence of the king, and said, "The secret which the king has demanded, the wise men, the astrologers, the magicians, and the soothsayers cannot declare to the king. But there is a God in heaven who reveals secrets, and He has made known to King Nebuchadnezzar what will be in the latter days. Your dream, and the visions of your head upon your bed, were these: As for you, O king, thoughts came to your mind while on your bed, about what would come to pass after this; and He who reveals secrets has made known to you what will be. But as for me, this secret has not been revealed to me because I have more wisdom than anyone living, but for our sakes who make known the interpretation to the king, and that you may know the thoughts of your heart" (Daniel 2:26-30 NKJV).

In Daniel 2:31-45, Daniel reveals the king's dream in great detail. In this dream God revealed the rising of future world powers to the current world powers. Most importantly in the dream, God through Daniel revealed

His kingdom and its complete sovereignty over all other kingdoms.

> *You, O king, were watching; and behold, a great image! This great image, whose splendor was excellent, stood before you; and its form was awesome. This image's head was of fine gold, its chest and arms of silver, its belly and thighs of bronze, its legs of iron, its feet partly of iron and partly of clay. You watched while a stone was cut out without hands, which struck the image on its feet of iron and clay, and broke them in pieces. Then the iron, the clay, the bronze, the silver, and the gold were crushed together, and became like chaff from the summer threshing floors; the wind carried them away so that no trace of them was found. And the stone that struck the image became a great mountain and filled the whole earth.*
>
> *This is the dream. Now we will tell the interpretation of it before the king. You, O king, are a king of kings. For the God of heaven has given you a kingdom, power, strength, and glory; and wherever the children of men dwell, or the beasts of the field and the birds of the heaven, He has given them into your hand, and has made you*

ruler over them all—you are this head of gold. But after you shall arise another kingdom inferior to yours; then another, a third kingdom of bronze, which shall rule over all the earth. And the fourth kingdom shall be as strong as iron, inasmuch as iron breaks in pieces and shatters everything; and like iron that crushes, that kingdom will break in pieces and crush all the others. Whereas you saw the feet and toes, partly of potter's clay and partly of iron, the kingdom shall be divided; yet the strength of the iron shall be in it, just as you saw the iron mixed with ceramic clay. And as the toes of the feet were partly of iron and partly of clay, so the kingdom shall be partly strong and partly fragile. As you saw iron mixed with ceramic clay, they will mingle with the seed of men; but they will not adhere to one another, just as iron does not mix with clay. And in the days of these kings the God of heaven will set up a kingdom which shall never be destroyed; and the kingdom shall not be left to other people; it shall break in pieces and consume all these kingdoms, and it shall stand forever. Inasmuch as you saw that the stone was cut out of the mountain without hands, and that it broke in pieces

> *the iron, the bronze, the clay, the silver, and the gold—the great God has made known to the king what will come to pass after this. The dream is certain, and its interpretation is sure* (Daniel 2:31-45 NKJV).

What the Lord did through Daniel was amazing! Without any prior knowledge of Nebuchadnezzar's dream, Daniel received revelation from the Lord describing the king's dream in detail along with its interpretation. Although we could comment about the meaning of the dream and the four kingdoms (Babylonian, Medo-Persian, Grecian, and Roman) that most scholars believe are represented in Daniel's interpretation, I would like to focus on the way Daniel responded throughout the process, particularly his interaction with Nebuchadnezzar in this instance.

The most important lesson we learn here from Daniel is to seize every opportunity to give God the glory and make Him known. Before Daniel began to reveal the dream to Nebuchadnezzar, he declared to the king there was a God in Heaven who was the Revealer of secrets. Always remember, God desires for people to know Him. Now, what was Nebuchadnezzar's response to Daniel's interpretation of his dream?

Then King Nebuchadnezzar fell on his face, prostrate before Daniel, and commanded that they should present an offering and incense to him. The king answered Daniel, and said, "Truly your God is the God of gods, the Lord of kings, and a revealer of secrets, since you could reveal this secret." Then the king promoted Daniel and gave him many great gifts; and he made him ruler over the whole province of Babylon, and chief administrator over all the wise men of Babylon (Daniel 2:46-48 NKJV).

They say that a picture is worth a thousand words. This picture of the king's reaction is priceless! The great Nebuchadnezzar, ruler of the most powerful kingdom in the world, falls on his face recognizing Daniel's God as the true God and promotes Daniel and begins to shower him with all manner of treasure. I can just see this rugged man of war with tears of joy in his eyes as Daniel disclosed the mysteries of Heaven to him. You can just imagine the anxiety and dismay lifting off him, being replaced by a smile.

This is why understanding dreams is so important. They have the ability to transform lives and lead people to the Lord as the Holy Spirit gives us the grace to interpret. Although King Nebuchadnezzar would need to go through a severe humbling experience later in his reign, he praised God and acknowledged that Daniel's God was above all other gods.

NEW TESTAMENT EXAMPLES

Joseph (Mary's husband)

Joseph of the New Testament arguably had the most impactful dream life of any person in the Bible. If there was ever anyone who needed direction and wisdom from a dream, it was Joseph. Though he was engaged to Mary, he was informed by his bride-to-be that she was already pregnant and the child was not his.

When we think about this amazing story, we sometimes examine it through a 21st-century lens. But if we look at the biblical account from the cultural perspective of Joseph living in Nazareth at around 4 BC, we can truly appreciate how extraordinary this man was.

For instance, in Jewish law an engaged or betrothed couple had a binding contract that was initiated before witnesses. Although the official wedding had not occurred, Joseph and Mary would have referred to each other as husband and wife. The betrothed couple abstains from sexual intimacy, and the bride stays at her father's house until the actual wedding ceremony. The betrothal contract could only be terminated by death or an official divorce decree.

In essence, Joseph and Mary were basically married "without benefits." So, based on the backdrop of cultural ramifications, Joseph's response to Mary's announcement of her pregnancy by the Holy Spirit is remarkable.

Joseph could have responded in anger by exposing Mary as a two-timing adulteress before divorcing her publicly and putting her life in jeopardy (see Deuteronomy 22:23-24). Can you imagine the conversation between Joseph and Mary? She had been away visiting her cousin Elizabeth for three months and showed up pregnant. His natural, logical conclusion would be that she had been unfaithful.

Joseph, however, takes a different approach—one of mercy. After having his entire domestic world turned upside down, Joseph decides to protect Mary by considering a secret divorce (Matthew 1:19). As Joseph contemplated the dilemma, God gave him a dream.

> But while he thought about these things, behold, an angel of the Lord appeared to him in a dream, saying, "Joseph, son of David, do not be afraid to take to you Mary your wife, for that which is conceived in her is of the Holy Spirit. And she will bring forth a Son, and you shall call His name Jesus, for He will save His people from their sins."

So all this was done that it might be fulfilled which was spoken by the Lord through the prophet, saying: "Behold, the virgin shall be with child, and bear a Son, and they shall call His name Immanuel," which is translated, "God with us."

Then Joseph, being aroused from sleep, did as the angel of the Lord commanded him and took to him his wife, and did not know her till she had brought forth her firstborn Son. And he called His name Jesus (Matthew 1:20-25 NKJV).

You can imagine Joseph's sheer joy after receiving the confirmation dream! Oftentimes, we people of God are perplexed and in need of wisdom about making difficult decisions. Dreams have the ability to confirm what the will of the Lord is in any given situation. In Joseph's case, he desperately needed reassurance to go through with his wedding plans. The dream was very direct in that the angel in the dream corroborated Mary's story, that she was indeed pregnant by an act of God the Holy Spirit, not by human means. Joseph desperately needed this assurance because what had occurred with his fiancé was beyond the scope of his experience and understanding.

Another important reason why the Lord reveals understanding to us in dreams is because sometimes His plans are so amazing and *otherworldly* that we need a supernatural encounter through a dream in order to wrap our minds around what He is doing in our lives.

Joseph had no reference point for a woman having a baby without a man. He needed an "anchor for his soul" (see Hebrews 6:19). God knows that we need this as well, especially if He is asking us to prepare for something that seems beyond the scope of our experience or current occupation.

For example, before I was called to serve at the church where I currently pastor, I was teaching as a professor at a Christian university. It had become apparent to my wife and me through prayer that God was going to transition us to another assignment. I assumed it would be to another Christian university, so we began to search for teaching jobs around the country.

As I continued to "burn up digital ink" by applying for university faculty positions, I started having recurring dreams about crossing a bridge over a body of water. The bridge did not look familiar to me at first. I then dreamed that I was preaching at a church I didn't recognize. It was at this point I received a phone call from a friend who lived in Maryland asking me to consider coming to interview for a senior pastor position; the church was in desperate need of leadership. Because of my recent dreams about preaching at a church, I contacted the district superintendent of this particular denomination.

As my wife and I drove from our townhouse in Virginia Beach, Virginia, to be interviewed by the elders and leadership, I noticed that the church building was exactly what I saw in my dream. Though I was aware that other pastoral candidates were applying for the senior pastor position, I knew I would be offered the position because God showed me beforehand.

Additionally, the recurring dream about the bridge and body of water turned out to be the Potomac River Bridge. This bridge spans the Potomac River from Charles County, Maryland, to King George County, Virginia. I recalled the dream as I was driving our rental truck across the bridge before moving into our new home in Maryland. I have had the privilege of serving at this church as the lead pastor for the past eleven years.

A Word of Caution

Before I move on to another New Testament dream example, I would like to give a word of advice and caution. The dreams that I have shared concerning how the Holy Spirit led my family to Maryland were indeed supernatural. I am forever grateful that God chose to confirm our assignment here. I do, though, want to caution my fellow dreamers that even though the Lord will use dreams to show you your future, warn you, or give direction, we must be careful not to get lazy in our prayer lives or reading of the Word of God. Please do not live your life solely based on dreams.

We must be led by the Holy Spirit. The Spirit of God will not tell us something that is contrary to the Word of God. Beware of counterfeit dreams from the enemy, which I will address in more detail a bit later in the book. If you stay in the presence of God and in His Word, you will be able to discern if a dream is coming from the devil.

Before we headed out to Maryland for our new assignment to pastor the church, we spent much time in prayer and in the Word inquiring of the Lord. The Lord confirmed what was in our hearts by giving the dreams. Although I was applying for teaching jobs, deep down inside I really wanted to pastor full time, but I had given this hope up to the Lord many years ago.

Also keep in mind that God is not limited to dreams. He can lead you through His Word, a friend, close family members, an angel disguised as a homeless person—any other way He chooses. We just need to keep our hearts open and our eyes on the Lord. He truly is our hope and anchor for our soul, firm and secure (Hebrews 6:19).

The Magi's Warning

One of the purposes of dreams is to warn us of impending danger. Such was the case when Jesus was just a baby. The wise men, or magi, were Eastern astrologers who had observed an unexplained phenomenon in the heavens, which they interpreted as a sign of the birth of the King of the Jews. The story of the wise men is chronicled in Matthew's gospel:

> *Now after Jesus was born in Bethlehem of Judea in the days of Herod the king, behold, wise men from the East came to Jerusalem, saying, "Where is He who has been born King of the Jews? For we have seen His star in the East and have come to worship Him"* (Matthew 2:1-2 NKJV).

Every time I read the Christmas story regarding the wise men, I am blessed because of the foreshadowing events surrounding the situation. In the story are Eastern astrologers who have traveled a great distance to inquire about a special baby. Religious leaders living in Jerusalem could have been searching for themselves based on all of the prophecies in the Old Testament. Instead, the coming of the magi and the disinterest of Jews in Jerusalem foreshadow the Gentiles' worship of the Messiah and the Jews' future outright rejection of Jesus, their Messiah (John 1:11).

God in His sovereignty utilizes the indifference of the religious leaders to keep the Messianic secret safe from the "false king," Herod the Great. God uses the power of the dream at this critical juncture in the young life of Jesus after the religious leaders confirm the birthplace of the Messiah to Herod.

> *Then Herod, when he had secretly called the wise men, determined from them what time the star appeared. And he sent them to Bethlehem and said, "Go and search carefully for the young Child, and when you have found Him, bring back word to me, that I may come and worship Him also."*
>
> *When they heard the king, they departed; and behold, the star which they had seen in the East went before them, till it came and stood over where the young Child was. When they saw the star, they rejoiced with exceedingly great joy. And when they had come into the house, they saw the young Child with Mary His mother, and fell down and worshiped Him. And when they had opened their treasures, they presented gifts to Him: gold, frankincense, and myrrh.*
>
> *Then, being divinely warned in a dream that they should not return to Herod, they departed for their own country another way* (Matthew 2:7-12 NKJV).

Although Matthew does not give specific details about the warning dream given to the wise men telling them not to return to Herod, we learn a lesson about radical obedience from these Eastern visitors. They were told by Herod to inform him once they had located the baby Jesus. Nevertheless, the magi were more concerned about obeying God than offending an earthly ruler.

Warning dreams like these are given so we can obey the Lord quickly with confidence. Though we don't have details about the dream, it must have provided a strong enough warning not to return to Herod.

I am reminded of a strong warning dream about a church that we attended many years ago when my wife and I had just become new parents to our firstborn baby girl. We had just transitioned from attending a large church and were considering making a particularly smaller ministry our new home church. We were actually friends with a married couple who were members of this church.

At first, we felt comfortable attending. The pastor had a prophetic calling on his life and he had given us prophetic words that we felt were from the Lord. As we continued to contemplate making this ministry our permanent home church, I had a warning dream one night from the Lord that I was not to join this local fellowship. My wife was in total agreement, especially since she began to trust my dreams track record. A few years later we learned from our friends who attended this church, that the pastor had multiple improprieties and decided to leave shortly after we did. We were so grateful that the Lord had warned us. We were able to avoid becoming entangled, delayed, and distracted.

BIBLICAL FRAMEWORK

Though I could share even more Old and New Testament dream examples in this opening chapter, these biblical dream samples were not meant to be exhaustive. They were to build a biblical framework so you can be confident knowing that God speaks through dreams and delights to reveal His will to us today through night visions.

Please continue with me on this dream journey as I record how the Lord has spoken through my dreams over the years. As you read about my dreams, dream symbols, their interpretations and subsequent fulfillment, it is my prayer you will be encouraged knowing how the Lord is speaking today and how He is speaking to you through dreams.

2

THE SEARCH FOR THE "JEWISH MOTHER"

I was working as an English teacher at a private Christian school in Virginia Beach, Virginia, as the primary breadwinner of our young family, shortly after the most horrific time in American history—9/11. Although I enjoyed teaching high school students, spending time with young people, and being called upon to preach every now and then at the weekly high school chapels, I had an overwhelming desire to be in full-time pastoral ministry.

One day I received a phone call from a lady who worked in the alumni and career office at the seminary from where I had graduated in 2000. The person on the other side of the phone would often contact former graduates from this particular university about possible ministry opportunities. I was elated when she informed me that there was an assimilation pastor from Illinois in town who was interested in meeting with me about potentially coming on staff at a megachurch.

I met him at a restaurant for brunch close to the beach called the "Jewish Mother." As we began to talk, two things became very clear right away. The first was that the food was amazing; and second, he had no interest in bringing on any new staff members at his church in Illinois.

Although I enjoyed the food, it seemed to be a waste of my time. I had agreed to meet him because I thought that I was about to be propelled into my dream of being in full-time pastoral ministry.

Almost twenty years later, I vaguely remember what we even talked about that day. It seemed he was just interested in taking an alum out for lunch. Disappointed and bewildered, I drove home to inform my wife. She encouraged my heart, as always. Little did I know at the time that God would use this experience and location—the Jewish Mother restaurant—to direct my steps through a dream.

Not long after this incident, my wife and I were seeking the Lord in prayer concerning leaving my job to begin a PhD program. I had been teaching high school during the day and moonlighting at night as a part-time Bible college instructor to earn extra money with, now, two babies in diapers. I discovered that I enjoyed teaching at the college level, but the doors were not open for full-time instructor work because I didn't have a terminal degree. It was a big decision because I would have to leave my teaching job of three years to become a full-time PhD student in addition to finding a part-time gig on campus to make it all work.

What were we going to decide?

I began to contemplate different scenarios. One option was to try and keep my job at the high school and still be a PhD student. This, however, was not realistic because I actually had to be on campus in class, which conflicted with my teaching schedule. I then contemplated staying on for another year at the high school, playing it safe and delaying my enrollment into the PhD program to provide finances for our growing family. As I began to lean more toward staying at my job because of complications and financial risks in venturing out, the Lord gave me what I label as a "direction/wisdom dream" revealing His will and my heart in the matter.

DREAM

I dreamed one night that I was riding on a bus with a group of people, and we were looking for the Jewish Mother restaurant. After driving around for an extended period of time, frustration began to set in because we had not located the restaurant. All of sudden, I suggested to everyone that we "just head to McDonald's," and the dream ended.

INTERPRETATION

Buses in dreams usually refer to a church, ministry, or a vocation of some sort depending on the context in a dream. Context is extremely important as it relates to understanding our dreams. My wife and I were seeking the Lord for direction regarding the timing to leave my job to start the PhD program. The fact that the Jewish Mother restaurant was in the dream was significant because I felt the same kind of frustration in the dream that I experienced after spending time with the assimilation pastor from Illinois.

At the time of my actual meeting at the restaurant, I thought I was going to be changing my vocation from schoolteacher to serving as a full-time pastor on staff. In the dream the Jewish Mother was now representing a transition into another vocation—full-time PhD student. What I said at the end of the dream was very important. In actuality, anytime there is any kind of talking part in a dream, we must pay close attention because God may be revealing your heart, His heart, or another person's heart to you. The fact that I encouraged everybody on the bus to settle for McDonald's was essential to understanding the dream, particularly in my personal context.

I never really liked McDonald's, so to suggest this restaurant in a dream was totally out of character for me. In the natural, I would not suggest it because I try not to eat fast food if I can avoid it. As I began to pray about the dream, the Lord showed me that McDonald's in the context of my dream represented my current vocation and venturing out into the unknown PhD program was represented by the Jewish Mother where I would have to trust God to open more doors financially.

Was I going to play it safe or take a risk?

The Lord revealed to me that I was acting out of character by not trusting Him to work things out. We decided to resign from my teaching position and start the PhD program.

While attending school as a full-time PhD student, in my second semester the Lord opened the door on campus for a full-time faculty position with the university. I was now able to attend class, teach in the undergraduate program in the evening, and get my work done in my office on campus. I am grateful for the Lord's direction through a dream. Also, I am now forever thankful for the "Jewish Mother."

3

THE BANQUET TABLE AND RICHARD PRYOR

For many years, particularly in the 1970s and '80s, the name Richard Pryor went hand and glove with stand-up comedy. The late comedian, entertainer, and actor had a long illustrious career filled with controversy, especially over his drug use.[1] At the time of his death, he was reportedly worth over $40 million. As a young person growing up in New York, Richard Pryor was a household name, especially in my family.

As a young boy growing up in Illinois, Pryor endured a family life that no child should ever have to experience. He was basically raised in his grandmother's brothel. His mother was a prostitute and his father was a bartender and former boxer. Due to Pryor's environment, he was also sexually abused. With such a horrific childhood, the only thing Pryor took solace in was his interest in movies. Considered a class clown, he discovered his talent in the arts and began acting in his early teens.

Though he started out as a "clean" comedian, Pryor gained his popularity because of vulgarity on stage and in his movies because he poked fun at the White establishment and traversed the racial divide. Despite his X-rated content and persistent substance abuse, he became one of the highest paid African American actors in the 1980s.

Why spend so much time talking about the life of a man like Richard Pryor? He was a very talented man. Unfortunately, he was remembered by those who knew him for having stormy relationships on and off stage, along with his frequent drug use. As much as Pryor was an American success, he was also an American tragedy. Several days before his death in December 2005, I had a prophetic dream about him that forever transformed my understanding of the depths of God's love.

Dream

In the opening scene of the dream, I am with actor and comedian Richard Pryor. We began to travel to different locations as they appeared to represent key moments in his life. I had the feeling like I was the "ghost" of Christmas past, present, and future, similar to Charles Dickens'

Ebenezer Scrooge. It was clear that I was sharing the gospel with him in every place we visited.

It seemed as if we were traveling for hours until we finally came to our last destination. We arrived at an exceptionally long banquet table topped with delicious-looking food. I turned to Richard Pryor and said, "Okay, Richard, how about it?" Pryor responded, "I don't know, man." The dream ended after he made this statement, and I woke up.

INTERPRETATION

This dream was actually one of my favorites of all time because it dealt with preaching the gospel—something I love to do. I was stunned when several days later on December 10, 2005, we learned that Richard died of a heart attack in Los Angeles. The dream was so real to me. I actually felt as if I had been awake talking all night. Was it more than a dream? Did God actually, supernaturally have me leave my body to preach the gospel to a dying Hollywood star? Fifteen years later I am still in awe about what really happened that night.

Though I may not be certain if I was in the body or out of it that night, I have no doubt that this was a prophetic/warning dream. Pryor's struggles in life have already been well-documented. I believe that the Holy Spirit was giving me a heads-up that eternity was hanging in the balance for Richard. The "ghost of Christmas" theme was a clear signal that Richard Pryor was close to departing the earth and needed to make a radical change by receiving Christ as his Savior. The huge banquet table represented the marriage supper of the Lamb where those who have put their trust in Jesus will be invited to dine as honored guests. The following is a wonderful example of this scene in the book of Revelation:

> *"Let us be glad and rejoice and give Him glory, for the marriage of the Lamb has come, and His wife has made herself ready." And to her it was granted to be arrayed in fine linen, clean and bright, for the fine linen is the righteous acts of the saints. Then he said to me, "Write: 'Blessed are those who are called to the marriage supper of the Lamb!'" And he said to me, "These are the true sayings of God"* (Revelation 19:7-9 NKJV).

Dismissing night dreams, especially ones about famous people, would be easy. Famous actors, politicians, and entertainers, however, need the Lord too—and God wants us to intercede for their salvation. I encourage you to be quick to pray for any public figure should the Lord prompt you.

The dream about Richard Pryor changed my life and gave me more confidence in the love of God for the lost. If Richard made the choice to sit at God's table, I look forward to our reunion one day in Heaven.

NOTE

1. Biography.com editors, "Richard Pryor Biography," The Biography.com website, A&E Television Networks, April 2, 2014, https://www.biography.com/performer/richard-pryor; accessed September 17, 2021. Pryor had a long history of substance abuse; he was severely burned over 50 percent of his body by a cocaine freebasing fire incident in 1980.

4

HOLDING
HANDS WITH MY
FUTURE BRIDE

It was the year 1998 and I was working on my Master's degree in seminary. I had graduated two years prior with my undergraduate degree and was serving as a youth pastor and itinerant preacher. I had just made a difficult decision to break up with a young lady I was dating while attending undergrad in Columbia, South Carolina. It was a grueling decision to end the relationship, but the Lord had confirmed several times she was not the one. The Lord even spoke a word about my future spouse at my ordination service before I traveled to Virginia Beach to begin my Master's program.

My Ordination Service

Several hours before my ordination service I was excited. I was about to graduate from Bible college in a few months and had invited my girlfriend—whom I believed at the time would be my wife—and her father to the special service. They traveled two hours from where my college was located to the church; her father was actually a professor at the school.

The little country church where I had served as a youth pastor during my time studying for the ministry was packed that night. My bishop had come to preach and ordain me. I was a bit nervous all night because he was very prophetic, and I knew that sometime during the evening he would have a word for me. I wanted things to go smoothly.

The ceremony actually did go smoothly. We had a great service. The worship was powerful and my bishop preached a wonderful message. We finally reached the part of the service for the official ordination ceremony, and the bishop began to prophesy an encouraging word over me. He was about to finish speaking and complete the ceremony when all of sudden he turned toward me, facing away from the audience with a piercing look in his eyes. I knew that look. I had seen it before. I call it the "read-your-mail" look.

The Holy Spirit had just spoken to him about me and relayed the following message: "Not long from now, a woman of purity is coming into your life." Most young Christian men about to graduate from college who receive a word like this would have been elated. I, however, was not. Didn't God realize that my current girlfriend and her father traveled two hours to support me? I felt like someone on one of those old Southwest Airlines commercials who just "wanted to get away" immediately from an embarrassing situation.

How was I going to respond to the word of prophecy just spoken over my life? If I were running for best actor that evening, I would have received the Oscar for best performance in a church service. After hearing my bishop prophesy about my future bride, I just smiled, but no one knew about the volcanic eruption taking place in my heart. Things had been going well at the time with my current girlfriend, and now I was somewhat unsettled after the service. I even began to reason in my mind that my girlfriend was the woman of purity about whom my bishop was talking. But in my heart of hearts, I knew he was talking about someone else.

After staying in the relationship for several more months, it started to become clear to my girlfriend and me that we were not as spiritually compatible as we thought. After much prayer we mutually agreed to end the relationship.

Pretty Woman and the Wrong Door

I was in my first semester of graduate school on the campus of Regent University in Virginia Beach. I had made an inner vow to myself that I was going to be committed to the Lord and my studies. In my mind, I was through with relationships for a while, especially since my heart needed time to heal from the last one. I had no clue that I was about to have a brief encounter with the woman of my dreams as I walked to the school library on that fateful day.

When I opened the door to enter the building, I saw a beautiful woman walking toward the door. She was wearing a pretty dress with a flowery pattern. I waited as she approached the door and held it open for her. As I patiently waited for her to exit the building, she went through the door next to the one I had been holding open for her. When she noticed that I was holding the other door open, she smiled at me apologetically. I just smiled and said, "No problem." It was an awkward moment and yet a cute one at the same time.

Though I continued to go about my day, I said to myself, *She's pretty, but I'm staying focused on my studies.* I meant what I vowed earlier. I was against pursuing a new relationship. In hindsight, the encounter was actually loaded with prophetic undertones. For many years I thought this young, beautiful woman—who would soon become my wife—made a mistake by going through the wrong door, but she recently revealed to me that she went through the other door on purpose. At the time, she was in another relationship—the wrong relationship. The prophetic irony was that the right door was the one I was opening for her, but because she was attracted to me, as she would admit later, she chose to walk on the other side.

Though I was resistant to a new relationship and she was dating the wrong guy, the Lord broke through our barriers. She ended her relationship with the person she was seeing, and we began dating a few months after the initial encounter. Although I had fallen in love with her, I had obstacles to overcome. My parents were divorced, and I knew this relationship was leading to marriage. Deep down inside I was afraid of marriage and wanted to know if she was the woman my bishop prophesied about at my ordination service a year prior. As I was seeking the Lord about these things, the Lord gave me a dream about her.

DREAM

One night I dreamed that I was holding hands with my girlfriend. The interesting thing about this dream was that we were suspended in the air high above a huge crowd of people in a big church. We were happy and very much at peace.

INTERPRETATION

An essential component to interpreting any dream is the context. In my particular context, I was working on my Master's degree in seminary in preparation for pastoral ministry. I was also praying for direction about the relationship that I was in and whether the woman I had fallen in love with was the one God had chosen to be my wife. The dream confirmed that April was the woman of purity that my bishop prophesied I would meet soon, and the church building represented the calling of God to serve together in pastoral ministry in the near future.

We have been happily married now for twenty-one years and we have two wonderful children! We also serve together as senior pastors in the church. She is literally the "woman of my dreams."

5

WHY AM I
DREAMING ABOUT
RONALD REAGAN?

Have you ever dreamed about a famous person? Many of us have had dreams about famous actors, singers, politicians, or Christian leaders. Should we just chalk these kinds of dreams up to our admiration for these kinds of people, too much pizza the night before, or an encounter with the Holy Spirit in the night?

The 2016 presidential election cycle pitted former Senator and Secretary of State Hillary Clinton against businessman and entertainer Donald Trump. Many people did not really give Trump much of a chance to win the election. There were even several voices within the church world that prophesied a victory for Clinton. To be honest, I was with the majority of people who believed that Trump's chances of winning were slim to none. My position, however, changed after a dream I had about former President Ronald Reagan several months before the election.

DREAM

One night I dreamed that the former, late President Ronald Reagan was back in the White House serving as President of the United States.

INTERPRETATION

Dreams can be challenging at times to interpret. This one, however, was not one of them. The context of this dream was that the country was in the middle of a hotly contested election between Hillary Clinton and Donald Trump. Ronald Reagan was the 40th President of the United States of America. The fact that I dreamed he was back in the White House had more to do with what he symbolized.

Of the two candidates running for president at the time, Donald Trump ran on a platform similar to Reagan's. For instance, Reagan and Trump had the following things in common: they were both republicans, they were both entertainers, and they also ran on conservative platforms. After examining the similarities between

Reagan and Trump, it became clear that the Lord was revealing Trump would be elected.

A Last Word About Dreaming
of Famous People

In closing, some guidance will be helpful regarding dreams about famous people.

First, bathe the dream in prayer and ask God for wisdom. Look up the person's name, because the mystery of the dream may unravel in the meaning of the person's name.

Second, consider what the famous person symbolizes based on their profession, character, or personality.

For example, I had a dream in June 2009 that recording artist and Grammy winner Lionel Richie had died. I was sad when I woke from the dream and prayed for him. The next day after the dream, I was shocked like most of the world, to learn of Michael Jackson's death. Lionel Richie is alive today, but at the time of my dream, he represented an important figure in the music world. The Holy Spirit was prompting me to intercede by giving me the dream about musician Lionel Richie.

Last, the Lord may be revealing something to you about famous people because He really does want you to intercede for them. Either way, dream encounters are invitations to pray and intercede.

6

ARABLE!

As the proud parents of two wonderful teenage children, I always want the best for them. My wife and I pray for them almost every day. Although I am grateful that both of my children love the Lord and have their own relationship with Him, like most of us, they can be off course in their responses at times.

One day I found myself having to make more "course corrections" than usual regarding the way they responded to a particular situation. The majority of my dad talks usually end with me reminding them about character. As a father, I ask myself at times, *Are they really getting it?* I try to avoid worrying about their future, especially with so much Scripture admonishing us against worry. One night I had an encouraging dream about my children that delivered me from any concerns about God's hand on their lives.

Dream

I was in my house at the time and my son and daughter were with me. I turned to them and began to repeat an unfamiliar word. I loudly shouted, "ARABLE, ARABLE, ARABLE...!" The dream then ended with this word still on my lips.

Interpretation

Looking up the word *arable* in the dictionary, I discovered it had to do with "land that is suitable for growing crops." The Lord was basically showing me that my children were "getting it" and they were good ground for producing a great spiritual harvest in their lives.

Advice Regarding Words, Phrases, and Images in Dreams

This night vision was one of the most encouraging dreams I have ever had from the Lord. Notice that this was one of my shorter dreams with not much action going on. It is also interesting to note that sometimes a short "word-centered" dream can be more profound than one with many different scenes. This dream about my children centered on the word *arable*. Anytime a word is highlighted in a dream, pay close attention to it and study it. The Lord may be unlocking something in you related to your destiny.

In fact, it is important to take note of any words, phrases, short images, or talking parts in a dream. The Holy Spirit may be giving you a word of knowledge—supernatural knowledge given to you by the Holy Spirit about something you had not known previously—a warning, wisdom about something, prophecy, or a word of encouragement.

I remember having a short dream several years ago about women crying during a church service. The interesting thing about the dream was the context. I had been invited to speak at a local church close to my house several months prior. I was considering canceling at the time because I temporarily had to walk with a cane while awaiting a hip procedure. Still, I could not get the image of the "crying women in the church" out of my head. I knew in my heart that God was showing me the local church that had invited me to preach there.

I decided to go, cane and all. As I was nearing the end of the sermon, the Holy Spirit brought to my remembrance the women I saw crying in my dream. I asked the congregation to raise their hands if anyone had been crying lately. What happened next after I asked the question continues to bless my soul even to this current day.

Several people raised their hands who had been literally crying in secret to the Lord about their situations. As I began to minister to them at the altar, the glory of the Lord came into the place and people began falling down under the power of God in different areas of the sanctuary, without me even touching them. It was actually one of the most powerful services I have ever been a part of. People were healed emotionally and received a tangible touch from the Spirit of God.

In closing this chapter, never overlook the importance of a word, phrase, or image in a dream. Always investigate. You never know when God is giving you a word of knowledge in your dream or is revealing something essential to your future or someone else's.

7

JET SKIING WITH TWO HUGE ALLIGATORS

You can probably surmise by now that I am enamored with the way God speaks mysteriously in dreams. I have often spoken the following question to my wife before going to bed for the night, "What adventure will it be tonight?" I remember an "adventure" that occurred almost ten years ago when the Lord sent us to pastor a small church in Maryland.

FOOL'S GOLD

My wife and I had been sent on assignment to redevelop a church that had been in existence since 1971. We had been gradually making changes at the church that dealt with worship music selections, physical appearance of the building, and overall programming.

In every new job there is always a honeymoon period. This is a time that usually lasts for a maximum of three months before the new worker begins to endure some kind of criticism or begins to be treated like everyone else. This is also true of new pastors taking over redeveloping churches—existing churches in decline that need to be renewed. Such was the case when my wife, two kids, and I arrived in Bowie, Maryland, to accept the pastorate. The congregation welcomed us with open arms. We were nervous but thrilled to have the opportunity to pastor full-time in ministry.

My wife and I were not the only ones who were excited. There was much anticipation and excitement within the congregation as well. The church had been stagnant for several years and had seen better days as many people had come and gone. But all of that was changing. The congregation was so stirred that they began to invite their friends and neighbors to come and see their new pastor. The church began to grow and the finances began to increase. Even though I was thankful for the growth and financial blessings, something didn't feel right in my spirit. I didn't know then that what I was experiencing is what I now call "fool's gold."

The term "fool's gold" refers to the substance pyrite, a common mineral consisting of iron disulfide and is pale brass-yellow with a metallic luster. The mineral has often been mistaken for gold by many prospectors. Pastors must understand that they may go through brief periods in church revitalization that look like a genuine turnaround and church growth, only to discover beneath the surface that real change has not occurred.

My wife and I came in with a don't-rock-the-boat mentality. We wanted to fit in and try to acquiesce to the current structure of the house. We tried to make changes gradually as we began to cast a new vision for the church. The demographic in our community had radically changed to almost 50 percent African American, and the church had not done much in the way of reaching out to them.

We knew that we needed to make some changes if we were ever going to connect with the Black community. We began to pray that God would send more help to our worship team and give us a worship leader who had the giftedness to lead blended worship with what I called a "gospel twist." The church was multiracial, with me being the first Black pastor in its history. I wanted to make sure that our worship reflected the diverse culture of our community.

With a few notable exceptions in the ministry, things appeared to be going well. We seemed to be keeping our heads above water as first-time senior pastors. Our kids were happy with their new school and we loved our new house. What could go wrong? At this particular time, I had one of the most sobering dreams of my life.

DREAM

In the dream my wife and I were having a wonderful time jet skiing on a beautiful lake. We made it to the other side of the lake but turned around to discover two huge alligators eating everything in their path. They even chewed through the wooden pier on the other side of the lake. We were grateful that God protected us because we didn't know they were in the water while we were jet skiing.

INTERPRETATION

Jet skiing with my wife on the water meant that we were enjoying our life and sweet communion with the Spirit of God, but the Lord was alerting us to unseen dangers below the surface at the church where we had been sent to pastor. The two huge alligators represented hidden danger in the form of verbal attacks that were really going to hurt.

Shortly after the dream, my wife and I endured one of the worst verbal attacks from several people at the church that we ever experienced. We discovered that beneath the surface there was an undercurrent of resentment by some influential members about the changes we were making to the church. The complaints against us had to do with everything from music selection to leadership style. We had been sent to make changes and redevelop this ministry. We were now seeing why this church had to be redeveloped in the first place.

The alligators also represented demonic spirits that had access to this ministry due to a history of division and offense even from former pastors who left the church. When we were alone in the building, my wife and I both heard at different times invisible chains rattling.

As we continued to pray and stand our ground, the main culprits behind the verbal attacks eventually left the church. We were thankful that the Holy Spirit warned us beforehand about the upcoming attack so we were not taken off guard.

A Word About Alligators/Crocodiles

The dream I just shared with you was not the only one I ever had that included alligators. I have seen these reptiles in my dreams several times over the years. In every instance, shortly after having the dream, I was slandered in some way. I remember listening to the late seer-prophet John Paul Jackson mention that dreams about alligators usually mean someone has a "long tale." Jackson pointed out it was really a play on words, as dreams often are.

The alligator has a long tail, and so does the person the enemy is using to spread discord. They just have a different kind of tale. It is important to realize that whether you see alligators or crocodiles in your dreams, both usually represent demonic activity and slander that is just around the corner.

Do not be afraid; the Holy Spirit is alerting you to take authority over the enemy and fight. Your prayers can lessen the impact and duration of an attack or prevent it altogether.

8

A FISH, A CANNON, AND A BASEBALL DIAMOND

Baseball has been a permanent focus in the Fox family for many years. I remember the thrill of going to see the New York Yankees play as a little boy for the first time and then ordering my first hotdog at Yankee Stadium. Later, the experience made an indelible mark on my life as a young man. My love for baseball grew more and more as I played Little League baseball, high school baseball, and then with the American Legion baseball team as a teenager.

Although all those experiences were terrific, the greatest satisfaction I ever had in baseball was coaching my son's middle school baseball team to a championship just before he entered high school.

Why share so much about baseball? Clearly, it has been a lifelong passion of mine. I included my baseball background because—similar to the parables of Jesus who shared stories with people that related to their shared experiences in their cultural context—God still gives us messages in dreams that relate to what we like or are familiar with. The Holy Spirit often uses common, everyday things in the flow of life to speak to us in dreams. In my case, it happened to be baseball.

DREAM

The setting of the dream was on a baseball field, and I was the head coach. As the teams were preparing to start the game, we were interrupted by the sound of a cannon. The cannon was under the dirt on the baseball diamond in the infield. Instead of discharging cannonballs, the cannon was shooting hundreds of fish at a rapid-fire pace all over the baseball field.

INTERPRETATION

This is an encouraging dream about the coming great worldwide revival about which many people have prophesied. The baseball field represented the world similar to what the "field" represented in the parable of the soils. Jesus explained this parable to His disciples in

Matthew's gospel when they inquired about the meaning of the "tares of the field."

> *Then Jesus sent the multitude away and went into the house. And His disciples came to Him, saying, "Explain to us the parable of the tares of the field." He answered and said to them: "He who sows the good seed is the Son of Man. The field is the world, the good seeds are the sons of the kingdom, but the tares are the sons of the wicked one. The enemy who sowed them is the devil, the harvest is the end of the age, and the reapers are the angels"* (Matthew 13:36-39 NKJV).

Although the baseball field is an important symbol to the overall understanding of this dream, the fish being shot out of the cannon on the baseball field is definitely the high point. Fish belong in the water, not on a baseball diamond. Traditionally fish in dreams normally represent believers, conversions, or humankind as potential believers.[1]

In my particular context, the fish were being shot out of the cannon with such force and velocity that it was easy for me to surmise that this referred to revival. It also reminded me when Jesus told His disciples to cast their nets out for a catch. When they obeyed the word of the Lord, there was such a multitude of fish that they struggled to bring them on board (John 21:6). The fish were symbolic of the harvest of souls that the disciples would rake in soon after Jesus ascended to Heaven. Like these early disciples, the fish in my dream represented the same thing—a harvest of souls with world-transforming implications.

NOTE

1. Adam F. Thompson and Adrian Beale, *The Divinity Code to Understanding Your Dreams and Visions* (Shippensburg, PA: Destiny Image Publishers, 2011), Kindle.

9

WHITE POWDER ON MY SUIT

There are dreams that I classify as bizarre. Usually these kinds of dreams don't have any recognizable symbol to help decipher the meaning. There is no reference point for what you are seeing in your dream. If you have a dream that just seems too weird to take seriously, please write it down before deciding to toss it into your "pizza dream" category. The following dream is one that could mistakenly have easily been tossed in with the pizzas.

DREAM

I was attending a church service, sitting in a pew. I seemed to be enjoying the man's sermon who was preaching, when suddenly a Caucasian man came into the church and threw white powder on my turquoise suit. Needless to say I was not happy with what this man had done. The dream left me sitting in shock about the incident.

INTERPRETATION

Some dreams will not have an explanation until God is ready to reveal the interpretation to you. The context of this dream was in a church setting. When I had the dream, I was serving at a church as the youth pastor. One day we had a guest minister for a special service. The visiting minister began to share his testimony about drug abuse and gave a warning for those in attendance to leave cocaine alone. After he said this, the dream that I had about the White man throwing white powder on my suit in the church flashed in front of my mind.

Not long after the dream we discovered that the founding pastor of our church had a drug problem and was also involved in several levels of corruption. He eventually was sent to prison.

DIVINE FLASHCARDS

God is amazing! The dream I just shared and interpreted is indicative of the way God works many times to reveal the meaning of dreams to His people. If you have a dream like the one I had about something really strange, write it down. Pray over it. If you have no context for the dream, no recognizable dream symbols, or really no clue of the interpretation, just relax and wait on the Lord. He will reveal the meaning to you later like a "divine flash-card" that comes across your mind.

I label them divine flashcards because they are quick, mind's-eye visions that the Holy Spirit gives when you are awake to reveal and confirm the interpretation of the dream. Usually the flashcard or flashback comes after some kind of outward stimuli that the Holy Spirit uses to bring it back to your remembrance. You may feel as if you have been somewhere before. You probably were there in spirit but realize that it is not déjà vu—it's the Holy Spirit communicating with you.

10

OCTOPUS TENTACLES ON A PASTOR'S HEAD

Images in our dreams are sometimes so shocking that if we were to see them in the natural course of everyday life, they would leave us completely speechless. This was indeed the case for me over twenty-five years ago when I dreamed about a well-known televangelist who was preaching with octopus tentacles on his head!

DREAM

In my dream I was with a famous television preacher who had a powerful healing ministry. As he was preaching, I noticed that there were octopus tentacles on his head. I began to talk to this minister about basic doctrines of the Christian faith, but he started to shake his head in disagreement over the basic tenets of Christianity. I persisted in the dream by trying to convince him that I was telling him the truth. The dream ended with me trying to persuade him to change his mind. The pastor just kept shaking his head in disapproval.

INTERPRETATION

This dream was a prophetic warning that the television pastor was venturing into an area of false doctrine. The fact that he was disagreeing with me in the dream about the basic tenets of the faith was an important issue. Equally important in this dream was the symbol of the octopus tentacles on his head. The octopus tentacles on his head meant that his mind was under demonic attack, and he was being controlled by an evil spirit.

GROWING IN MATURITY

At the time of this dream, I had just been discharged from the military and was attending a wonderful Pentecostal church in North Carolina. I was living with my parents and contemplating going to Bible college. After I had the dream, the Holy Spirit led me to pray for the pastor who was in the dream. I wish that I could say I actually followed through on what the Lord instructed me to do. I didn't.

Rather, I actually did something that today I label immature. I told people in my church about my dream and this famous individual. Why did I do it? I guess in hindsight I wanted their affirmation as to whether or not I heard from God about this person. It did not go over well, however, when I shared my dream.

I noticed by the look on the people's faces that they were questioning my motive, perhaps thinking, *Who are you to say something about this great man?* Couldn't they discern that God was speaking to me? I went back to the Lord in prayer and heard, "I told you to pray for him, *not talk about him.*" I repented immediately.

Herein is an important lesson about dreams. Dreams are an invitation to intercede in prayer. Too many times immature seers, prophets, and other believers in general, rush to share every dream they receive with other people. Instead, we need to learn how to soak in the dream, pray for direction, or simply intercede before sharing it with others. If you do these things, the Holy Spirit will give you more dreams because you are trustworthy to pray and follow directions.

A Pastor Repents

What happened to the television pastor I dreamed about? I was elated one day when I sat down to watch his television broadcast and he told his viewing audience that he was wrong and had been in error. He repented over the airwaves. I learned later that a former mentor and seminary professor of mine, who is now in Heaven, was the one who corrected his theology.

This episode was important in my dream journey because it gave me confidence and yet humbled me at the same time. I now had assurance that God was actually speaking to me. Although I was young, inexperienced, and basically unknown, God revealed what was happening in the life of a famous pastor who lived hundreds of miles away from me. I was humbled that God chose me to intercede for this great man of God and allowed me to see him be restored.

11

WARFARE ON A SHIP

For we do not wrestle against flesh and blood,
but against principalities, against powers,
against the rulers of the darkness of this age,
against spiritual hosts of wickedness in the
heavenly places (Ephesians 6:12 NKJV).

Ephesians 6:12 declares that our fight is not against other humans but against the invisible forces of darkness that have infiltrated every sphere of society. Sometimes the Holy Spirit will show us just how intense the spiritual warfare is in our personal lives, in our communities, and in our world. I believe the next dream will encourage you to engage the enemy with boldness and clarity.

DREAM

In my dream I found myself walking through a certain neighborhood. As I strolled through this community, I sensed hopelessness. I observed people sitting on their front porches looking downtrodden and depressed. All of a sudden, the scene in the dream shifted to me on a ship at sea. I began to inspect the vessel and quickly discerned the feeling of spiritual bondage. I saw people who were physically sick, using drugs, and others who were involved in prostitution. It seemed I was on a demonic slave ship and the people were being used as demonic cargo.

I started to minister to the people and saw those with addictions suddenly set free. It was as though they were all standing in a line, and as I walked by them, I knew by the Holy Spirit what was wrong with them and gave each person words of knowledge. Some were instantly healed. I remember telling one lady that her kidneys would begin to function in a few days. It was awesome!

When I finished ministering to the people on the ship, I was getting ready to exit but I suddenly saw stairs leading up to the top of the ship where I imagine the captain's quarters would be. I decided to go up the stairs to investigate. When I entered the upper room of the ship, I saw a dark figure laying on a bed. As I looked more closely, I saw what appeared to be a naked muscular man sleeping. Immediately I was filled with righteous indignation because I instantly knew who this person was—the principality in charge of everything on the slave ship. He was responsible for all the pain and suffering happening down below. As he slumbered, I confronted him by demanding him to "Get up!" I had no fear whatsoever.

He got up quickly and lunged at me with tremendous force, but I blocked every blow he threw at me. I defended myself with such ease, as though I was an expert in karate. Eventually I knocked him to the floor. The battle was not over though.

I wondered if there was a Bible nearby I could use. As I turned to my right, I saw a small New Testament Bible on top of a piece of furniture. I quickly grabbed it and placed the New Testament Bible on the demonic entity's chest. As soon as the Bible touched him, he was totally defeated and the dream ended.

INTERPRETATION

Although this was a detailed dream and one of my longer ones, the meaning is fairly basic. The dream was an invitation to engage in spiritual warfare and fulfill the call of God on my life. The people on the slave ship are the people God is calling me to minister to in the future. He wants these people set free from the hand of the enemy. The Holy Spirit also gave a reminder that I was to follow the example of Jesus by defeating the enemy with the "sword of the spirit," which was represented by the small but mighty New Testament Bible that I placed on the chest of the principality. (See Ephesians 6:17 and Hebrews 4:12.)

A WORD ABOUT SPIRITUAL WARFARE IN DREAMS

From this night vision encounter, it is clear that a dream can be an invitation to engage in spiritual warfare. In this case, my dream about the slave ship was both an invitation and a confirmation of my calling to engage in spiritual warfare to set captives free. Dreams are so important that the Holy Spirit can use them as a springboard to mighty breakthroughs in the spirit realm that affect the natural realm.

The following is a good example from my book titled *Preparing for the Great Outpouring: Is Your Heart Ready for a Move of God?* where I quote author and prophetic intercessor Rebecca Greenwood:

> Because of my calling to deliverance, prophetic intercession, and strategic warfare prayer, there have been several instances when demonic entities have attempted to intimidate me from

advancing. In one such occasion, we were contending against the spirits behind abortion.... Wichita, Kansas, housed an abortion clinic run by a doctor who was viewed by the public and self-satisfied as America's most productive abortionist, Dr. George Tiller. In his lifetime work, he aborted no less than sixty thousand unborn infants. Abortions, including late-term abortions, were the only medical procedures he executed in his practice.

I returned in the fall of 2007, which proved to be a divinely appointed and orchestrated spiritual warfare assignment. For months, believers in the state had been aggressively researching and praying that the spiritual root or demonic principality behind the notorious abortion clinic would be exposed. In preparation for our coming prophetic act, we prayed, asking the Lord to disclose the stronghold. At that moment, the Lord remarkably brought back to my memory a dream I had in 1994 in which He revealed to me the demonic spiritual entity lilith. She is cited in Isaiah 34:14 as the night monster. The Hebrew word is lilim or lilith, whose name means the night monster, night hag, or screeching owl.... In the dream the

Lord expressly showed me this territorial deity
to be one of the principal forces behind death
and abortion.[1]

I included this story because it highlights the way the
Holy Spirit can use dreams in the life of a believer as a means
to spiritual breakthrough. Rebecca Greenwood's dream
about the territorial spirit lilith, mentioned in Isaiah
34:14, uncovered the forces behind abortion in Wichita, Kansas. Greenwood and her prayer team engaged the
principality over the abortion clinic. The clinic began to
encounter legal issues and eventually closed.

The warfare ship dream is simply a microcosm of
what I believe happens to believers worldwide as the
Holy Spirit calls the Body of Christ to action to engage
in the work of spiritual warfare.

Whether you have a dream of fighting on a slave ship
with a principality, find yourself being chased by thugs,
or dreaming of a huge, dark tornado coming over your
city, your response should always be grounded in prayer.
Fight the good fight of faith and stay persistent in prayer
until you sense the Holy Spirit give the "all clear."

And always keep in mind the following verse: *"...The
earnest prayer of a righteous person has great power and
produces wonderful results"* (James 5:16 NLT).

NOTE

1. Rebecca Greenwood, *Glory Warfare: How the Presence of God Empowers You to Destroy the Works of Darkness* (Shippensburg, PA: Destiny Image: 2018), Kindle Edition, 43-44, quoted in Charles R. Fox, *Preparing for the Great Outpouring: Is Your Heart Ready for a Move of God?* (Newberry, FL: Bridge-Logos Publishing, 2020), 86-87.

12

FLYING

I love heights! It doesn't matter if I'm flying on a plane, a helicopter, or riding the highest roller coaster, I like to be in the air. I also love "flying" dreams. What is wonderful about dreams is that natural laws such as gravity do not apply. These kinds of dreams can give a person an air of invincibility, like a superhero. After awakening from a flying dream, a sense of euphoria remains because I so much enjoy flying unassisted. I have had several dreams through the years about flying, and will go into more detail about their meaning later in this chapter. But for now, let's examine one of my more recent flying dreams.

DREAM

In my dream I was flying unassisted over water and feeling free. As I continued to fly, I heard the Lord say, "Test the limits and fly higher." I obeyed immediately and began to fly higher.

INTERPRETATION

This is a very encouraging dream from the Lord about going deeper into the Spirit in my personal walk with God. The fact that I was flying over water without needing to be in an airplane is significant because it means that I have the ability to move freely in the things of God. Flying over water can also refer to receiving revelation about the things of God, or in this instance, traveling "overseas" or internationally to do ministry.

Another important aspect of the dream involved the voice of the Lord telling me to "Test the limits and fly higher." My wife has a degree in film producing and has taught me a lot about certain protocols and nuances in the movie industry. One such detail is that no matter how small an actor's talking role is in a Screen Actors Guild (SAG) movie, the person can qualify to apply for membership in Screen Actors Guild. Being part of this guild is important for an actor because it gives the person credibility and benefits. Just like an actor with a talking role, dreams that have voices or talking parts should garner our undivided attention and qualify the dream for a thorough investigation of any words spoken.

The Voice in my dream instructed me to fly higher and test the limits. The fact that I was actually able to fly much higher in my dream with relative ease signified that I was maturing in my spiritual gifts.

When I woke from the dream, the movie *Man of Steel* was also on my mind. In this newer version of the DC comic superhero Superman, the film portrays the character's origin story. The character, Clark Kent, discovers that he is not human but a superpowered alien from the planet Krypton.

Unlike the older versions of the Superman series, the *Man of Steel* movie shows a more vulnerable side of Superman who has to master flying and even falls from the air one time as he learns how to fly. It is interesting that Superman's father tells him that he has grown strong, but the only way to know how strong is to keep testing his limits. In my dream, my heavenly Father was giving me the same kind of encouragement.

INSIGHTS ABOUT FLYING DREAMS

As I previously mentioned, natural laws like gravity don't apply in dreams. If you have had the privilege of earning "frequent flyer" status in dreams, you should be aware of a few things before your next "flight." The first understanding is that your ability to fly in dreams signifies you are moving freely in the Spirit and also in spiritual gifts.[1]

The late John Paul Jackson, seer and founder of Streams Ministries, made the following observations about those who frequently fly in their dreams:

> Dreamers who are "frequent flyers" will typically have some of the following spiritual gifts: The gift of prophecy or revelation (the supernatural enablement of the Holy Spirit to receive information from God that would be otherwise unknowable). The gift of discerning of spirits (the supernatural enablement of the Holy Spirit that allows a person to determine whether a spiritual manifestation emanates from God, the devil, the world, or man). Any other gift or combination of gifts of the Holy Spirit. It is also important to consider how skilled you were at flying in the dream. The quality and control of your flying will usually reference how mature you are in your spiritual gifts. Were you floating like a balloon? That likely means you've been given the supernatural ability to move in the spirit, but you haven't developed the maturity (training or discipline) to control it. Were you soaring like an eagle or hovering just off the ground? This could reference your gift's maturity as well, but it also might mean your area of authority or the

platform (the intersection of favor and opportunity) God is currently giving you.[2]

It is my prayer that wherever you are in your spiritual walk, you will be encouraged to go higher in the Lord. Having had the privilege of flying in my dreams through different seasons in my life, I am grateful for every one of these encounters. Whether I was barely off the ground or soaring in the air like an eagle, these dreams encouraged me to go after God more and produced more intimacy with Him.

Herein is the crux of the matter to any flying dream—intimacy with God! Although dreams of flying can reveal prophetic insight, maturity in your spiritual walk, or dexterity in the spiritual gifts, the most important takeaway is that God is madly in love with you and desires a deeper relationship with you.

Notes

1. Adam F. Thompson and Adrian Beale, *The Divinity Code to Understanding Your Dreams and Visions*, Kindle.
2. John Paul Jackson, *Top 20 Dreams: What the Most Common Dreams Are Telling You* (Lewisville, TX: Streams Ministries, 2015), Kindle.

13

THE WASP AND THE HAMMOND B3 ORGANS

It has been said that "Jesus is the reason why people enter the pastorate, but conflict is why many leave the pastorate." As a person who has been in ministry for more than twenty-six years and a senior pastor for eleven years, I can fully attest to the veracity of this statement. Conflict has sent many pastors permanently out to pasture.

In my experience, the area of ministry where I have observed the most conflict has been in the music ministry. As I have interviewed various pastors over the years, many have testified that most of their problems stem from the music ministry. I believe satan loves to attack this important ministry in the church because he wants to steal our worship. He hates when we worship our God.

As mentioned previously, my wife and I were sent to redevelop a church in Bowie, Maryland.

To no surprise, one of our biggest challenges in this ministry centered on worship. I received the following warning dream regarding the music ministry shortly after I became the pastor.

DREAM

The setting of the dream was in a church service and there were two huge organs on the platform. Both organs looked like Hammond B3 organs and were being played wonderfully by two young African American men. As I was standing there enjoying the music, a huge wasp came out of one of the organs and stung me on the side of the neck. It was painful.

INTERPRETATION

The dream about the two oversized Hammond B3 organs was an important warning dream centered on my current situation regarding music ministry at our church. We had been praying that God would send us an anointed worship leader who could play the keyboard and also help transition the congregation into a more blended style of worship with an emphasis on Black gospel.

The reason why I believe the Lord showed me the two oversized organs was to alert me to the demonic stronghold in my region that was responsible for the music culture in the churches in my area. Wasps in dreams usually represent high-ranking evil spirits.

Before I had the dream, I was thinking of hiring a musician from one of the neighboring churches to play Black gospel music because I wanted to reach African Americans in our community. Now that I look back on the situation, the real issue was not about getting a Black sound, White sound, or contemporary sound—I was after a "Kingdom sound."

The Holy Spirit was showing me that my decision to hire talent from the outside was going to sting me. I learned later that there were many musically gifted hirelings in my region. I needed to be patient and trust the Lord to raise up the right person.

After the dream, I decided to wait on making a move on the worship team front. Eventually the Lord did send us a wonderful worship leader who was classically trained on the piano. He made a huge impact in the church and was with us for several years. He was with us until he was married and later called to pastor a church in a neighboring city in the state. After his departure, I wish I could tell you that I adhered to the advice of the Holy Spirit and was patient.

As time went on, I neglected to keep the warning dream at the forefront of my mind. I wanted to replace the worship leader so I started to look for someone to fill his position. I failed to realize that God had sent us the last worship leader and He could have also provided another one in His own time. Nevertheless, I rushed to fill a need in our ministry—and quickly went through four worship leaders in a span of three years because I didn't adhere to the warning dream.

To my utter shock and dismay, I was stung on the neck by an actual wasp when I walked out of my house one day in the summer to sit on my front porch. As I ran back into the house to tell my wife and seek help, I was brought back to my dream regarding the oversized Hammond B3 organs. The pain from the wasp sting further reinforced my commitment to follow the leading of the Holy Spirit in all matters. My frustration with the music ministry could have been avoided if I had heeded His warning.

KEEPING WITH OBEDIENCE

The dream about the musical organs underscores the need to stay obedient. I initially followed the leading of the Holy Spirit by waiting on God to send the right person to our church to lead worship. The Lord graciously answered my prayer. I began to have trouble by making the same mistake that Paul accused the Galatians of making: *"How foolish can you be? After starting your new lives in the Spirit, why are you now trying to become perfect by your own human effort?"* (Galatians 3:3 NLT).

In this verse, Paul defends the gospel by reminding the Galatians that their Christian life started with faith in the crucified Jesus Christ and was validated by the gift of the Holy Spirit. The apostle admonished them that it would be foolish to abandon God's way to try and reach maturity through their own efforts.

Like the Galatians, I had a great start but quickly abandoned the warning that the Lord gave about the direction of the ministry. I did not stay in obedience. This episode in my life taught me a valuable lesson that has stayed with me regarding spiritual intensity.

Once the Lord reveals His will to you whether through a dream, a rhema word, prophetic utterance, or by some other means, He wants you to maintain your spiritual intensity with radical obedience until He gives further instruction. I am reminded of King Saul and the prophet Samuel in the Old Testament. Saul was given specific instructions by the Lord through Samuel. Saul only partially obeyed the Lord and suffered drastic consequences for his disobedience.

Samuel also said to Saul, "The Lord sent me to anoint you king over His people, over Israel. Now therefore, heed the voice of the words of the Lord. Thus says the Lord of hosts: 'I will punish Amalek for what he did to Israel, how he ambushed him on the way when he came up from Egypt. Now go and attack Amalek, and utterly destroy all that they have, and do not spare them. But kill both man and woman, infant and nursing child, ox and sheep, camel and donkey.'" ...But Saul and the people spared Agag and the best of the sheep, the oxen, the fatlings, the lambs, and all that was good, and were unwilling to utterly destroy them. But everything despised and worthless, that they utterly destroyed (1 Samuel 15:1-3,9 NKJV).

Saul eventually lost his kingdom and his life in battle. Though our acts of disobedience do not usually garner the kind of tragic consequences that Saul endured, they nonetheless leave us open to demonic attack and delay the blessings of the Lord in our lives. In this story in First Samuel 15, Saul would be confronted by the prophet Samuel about his "selective" obedience and rebellious heart (see 1 Samuel 15:10-34).

In closing, if this chapter is prompting you to reevaluate an area of your life where you know that God has given you specific instructions, you can repent and tell your heavenly Father right now that you are sorry. He wants you to get back in step and go back to the last thing He told you—and just do it!

14

MY BIG BROTHER IN HEAVEN

More than thirty years ago I received the news that no family member ever wants to hear about their sibling. My father informed me after I arrived home from my part-time job at the grocery store that my big brother Derrick had been killed. Even now, writing about this thirty-two years later, I still get a little emotional when I think about that fateful night. I was only seventeen years of age and he was just twenty.

I loved my older brother, but his drug problem had put a strain on our relationship. My parents had really been at their wits' end with him because of the way his substance abuse had affected all of our lives. Derrick was a talented football player in high school and was being recruited to play as a linebacker in college. Unfortunately, he dropped out of school and began to associate with the wrong people. He eventually started selling drugs and became addicted to cocaine.

Although we were both raised in a Christian home, my brother struggled with addiction. Yet Derrick would demonstrate from time to time his biblical foundation by making profound statements for a young man his age. I remember a conversation about prayer that we had before going to bed one night. I was tired and ready to go to sleep but my brother asked me if I had said my prayers before I climbed up to the top bunk. I told him that I said my prayers while lying in bed.

He told me, "God is a King and you need to get down on your knees when you pray." Though there are many different postures in prayer, what Derrick said that day has stayed with me. His statement represented a divine awareness and respect for the Lord—one that is often lacking in certain church environments where respect for the majesty of God has been trivialized.

As I reflect on the statement that my brother made about prayer, I am reminded of the biblical truth that no matter what we see on the outside of a person, God is the One who really knows what is happening in their hearts (see 1 Samuel 16:7). Regardless of his shortcomings and addiction, my big brother Derrick had a heart of gold and would give the shirt off his back to those in need.

Unfortunately, he made poor choices that cost him his life. After his death, our family was devastated. Though his death was the hardest I had ever experienced in my young life, the most difficult was not knowing if he made it to Heaven. Was my brother all right? Was he being comforted or was he in torment?

As time went on and after moving with my family from New York City to a small town in South Carolina, the Lord gave me a dream that eradicated my doubts and questions about the whereabouts of my big brother.

DREAM

In my dream I was walking in a beautiful green meadow, and in the distance I saw my brother Derrick standing under a tree. I ran to him and hugged him tightly. I told him that I really missed him. We walked together and he spoke to me about God's intentions for humankind. He told me that God's desire was always to dwell and fellowship with His creation. I was stunned by what my brother said and the way he said it—his speech was different from how he spoke when he was on earth. There, he was a man of the streets and used urban slang most of the time. Not only was there a difference in his speech, but he looked great. I knew that he was at total peace with himself.

INTERPRETATION

The dream I had about my brother was a healing dream that bought comfort and confirmation. The Lord confirmed my questions as to the whereabouts of my big brother. My concern for his soul was now alleviated because I saw him alive in what I believe was Heaven. The dream not only bought comfort but also closure as I was given the opportunity to talk to my brother one last time.

It is my sincere prayer that this story about my brother will comfort you if you have lost a loved one. The dream about my brother not only brought incredible peace to me, but it blessed others in my family as well. Although I didn't ask for a healing dream about Derrick, the Lord was gracious to me. I believe God will do the same for you. I close with the words of the apostle Paul:

> *Blessed be the God and Father of our Lord Jesus Christ, the Father of mercies and God of all comfort, who comforts us in all our tribulation, that we may be able to comfort those who are in any trouble, with the comfort with which we ourselves are comforted by God* (2 Corinthians 1:3-4 NKJV).

15

A STUDENT'S NEED

As mentioned in a previous chapter, the Holy Spirit can give you a word of knowledge in your sleep. Many years ago when my children were just toddlers, I worked as a teacher in a Christian private school in the daytime and moonlighted by teaching at a local Bible college close to our house in the evening. After returning home from my daytime teaching job, I would usually take a nap before heading out again for my second job. One day I had a short dream while resting before work in the evening.

DREAM

In the dream encounter I recognized a student in my class. He seemed distraught and was in tears as he was crying out to God in prayer in his home. He could not see me in the dream. I was just an observer. The student said the following that gripped my heart, "I have nothing to eat." I woke up after this.

INTERPRETATION

Though many of the dreams I have are metaphorical in nature, requiring prayer and research. This one turned out to be literal. The Lord gave a word of knowledge about the current need of a student in my class who had fallen on hard times financially. Notice that I was just an observer in the dream, not the focal point.

To be grammatically correct, every sentence must have a subject, verb, and complete idea. Similarly, every dream has a subject. One thing I have learned about interpreting dreams over the years is if you determine the subject of the dream, it becomes easier to interpret. If you can take yourself out of the equation in the dream, would the dream still make sense? If it does, there is a good chance that you are not the subject of the dream. In my dream, my student was the subject.

What was I to do?

The first thing I did—and what you should always do about any dream—was pray about it. Even if you think it is an easy dream to interpret, always ask the Holy Spirit for guidance. His plan may be different from your plan.

At the time of the dream, my wife and I had two young children and money was tight, especially on a private Christian schoolteacher's salary as our primary source of income. I could have just prayed in secret for the student. I could have prayed for God to meet his need. Yet, after praying, I sensed that God wanted me to do more than pray. My wife and I prayed and agreed to sow a seed of twenty dollars, which was a stretch for us at the time, into his life.

When I arrived at class that evening, I found the student before class and discreetly gave him the twenty-dollar bill. He responded to my gift with the following words, "Now I know that you hear from God."

I believe this story underscores the importance of following the leadings of the Holy Spirit. The dream not only built up the faith of this student, it built my faith as well. Although I only had twenty dollars to give, money served as a sign to the Bible college student that God had heard his prayer and that the Lord was going to provide for him. I was encouraged in my faith to walk in more boldness because of the outcome of the situation.

When we walk in obedience by following the promptings of the Holy Spirit through dreams, visions, impressions, or through the Word of God, the Holy Spirit will reveal even more truth and direction to us because He can trust us to not only pray but to act!

16

THE UPROOTED TREE

A few years ago, I started attending a monthly prayer group for pastors and church leaders. Each month the prayer meeting would rotate to a different church. I really enjoyed the fellowship. As I continued to attend the prayer group, I began to develop solid relationships with some of the leaders that I am still grateful for even to this day.

On one Sunday as service began at the church that I pastor, one of the men from my prayer group entered the building with his two adult sons. It was a nice surprise. I was happy to see him. After service he mentioned that he wanted to make our ministry his new church home and that he wanted to serve. I was intrigued, particularly because he had previous ministry experience helping other churches in the city. I was also interested in him because he was White and our church was predominately African American. We could really use the diversity, especially with the vision I had of a multicultural congregation.

After finishing our new-member orientation, I appointed the man and his wife to serve in our Sunday school ministry. They had years of Bible teaching experience in other churches, so I felt they would be a good fit. Things ran smoothly at first and there was much excitement over our new adult Sunday school teachers.

As time went on, the family became a permanent fixture in the life of the church. The gentleman even helped repaint the lines in our parking lot and also helped us stay up to date on our building code with our city by planting trees on the islands in our parking lots. I began to strongly consider him to be an elder until I had a dream one evening.

DREAM

In my dream I was in our church parking lot. Suddenly I saw one of the trees planted by our adult Sunday school teacher be completely uprooted and fall into the kitchen of a house on the church property.

INTERPRETATION

I would classify this as a warning dream. Our Sunday school ministry department was going well, and I was getting ready to recommend the Sunday school teacher to be appointed as an elder in our church. But, the dream about the uprooted tree that he planted stopped me in my tracks.

Trees in dreams can have different meanings depending on the context. The fact that this man had just established "new roots" by becoming part of our ministry was significant, especially considering the fact that trees in dreams typically refer to people. (See Psalm 1:3; Isaiah 7:2; 61:3; Jeremiah 17:8.)

Although the ministry was going well at that moment, the fact that the tree planted by this individual was uprooted indicated that his ministry at the church would be short-lived. After the dream I decided to wait on making the man an elder so I could watch his life a bit more closely. Eventually, I began to see character flaws. He began to do things at the church that caused concern.

For example, one Sunday after service he came to me and criticized everyone in the worship service, informing me privately that the members of our church had a sense of entitlement. He also began to make physical changes to the fellowship room where he taught without getting my permission. In actuality, I discovered that he had another vision for the church that conflicted with mine, the senior pastor.

It also became known that he and his wife were having marital trouble. He portrayed a good relationship at church, but that relationship was not his reality at home. All of these concerns climaxed as we were preparing to celebrate Black History month the last Sunday in February.

Our youth group had a special dance prepared and they had worked tirelessly to do a good job. I was stunned when I received an email from this brother on the Friday before the Sunday service telling me that he had concerns about our Black History month presentations. He informed me in the email that he was "very offended by last year's presentation" and that he didn't want to sit through it again.

Though I tried to explain it was never our intention to offend him but to promote unity in the Body of Christ by celebrating our diversity, he was not convinced. I even offered him the opportunity to come meet with my wife and me to discuss his concerns.

Sunday arrived and we decided to go on with the presentation. The youth did a fantastic job and people in the church were blessed by them. The adult Sunday school teacher, however, was not happy with the performance. We had scheduled a meeting with him and his wife immediately after service that day to discuss his concerns. I was surprised that his wife was the only one to come meet with us; he decided to skip our meeting.

This is when his wife revealed he had been verbally abusive to her and their children in the past. She also told us that he was a bully and struggled with issues of racism. My wife and I sat there in utter shock over what she was saying. We really felt for her because we could see the pain on her face from all she had suffered in the marriage.

Her husband portrayed a totally different persona at church than he did at home. As she sat in my office sharing these concerns about her husband, he called her on her cell phone from the church parking lot. We overheard him threatening to leave her there if she didn't walk out of my office and get in the car.

Though she decided to heed his threats by walking out to the car, it was too late. The secret life of this man was out in the open. I set up a meeting with him during the week to lovingly confront him about what happened on Sunday and to offer my help with the marital issues. During our meeting, he doubled down on his disapproval of the Black History program and also voiced his criticism for the youth of our church. Though we tried to confront him with the love of Jesus, he decided to turn in his keys and leave our church.

A little over five months after this incident, I was informed by a friend that the man died due to complications from prostate cancer. I was stunned at the news and thought about the dream of the uprooted tree that he planted. I immediately thought about the following verse in Matthew 15:13 (NKJV) when Jesus was alluding to the Pharisees: *"But He answered and said, 'Every plant which My heavenly Father has not planted will be uprooted.'"* Though I was saddened by the way the man left the church and his subsequent death, the ordeal left me astonished at the way the Lord revealed the future to me.

After his passing, his wife informed me that before her husband died, he apologized to her for things he had done in their marriage. With tears in her eyes, she spoke about his last days in the hospital when he apologized to her for treating her poorly. Toward the end he was a much different man, reminding her of the man she fell in love with many years ago. What made the difference in this man's life? Was it simply the fact that he wanted to get right with God because eternity hung in the balance? Possibly.

I, however, believe it was a combination of factors. I believe a larger, more eternal picture exists than just what happened at our church. The prophetic dream prompted us to start praying for him because the Lord wanted to make sure this man repented of his sins before meeting his Maker. I believe our prayers in response to the dream flushed out what was really happening in this man's life to prepare his heart for eternity.

17

Lightning from Heaven on a Dark Road

There are certain events in our Christian walk that become watershed moments we can always go back to when our faith is tested. Perhaps it was a time when the Lord made a financial path where there was no way, or when you received an unexpected check in the mail before your car was about to be repossessed. Maybe it was a miracle of healing for a loved one when doctors gave little chance for survival. I could go on and on about the miraculous power of God and His wonderful faithfulness.

Experiencing God in these ways leaves us with testimonies we can stand on when we encounter future challenges. I have several stories of God's faithfulness through the years, but there is one special dream encounter I go back to when I need more confidence than usual. In this night vision, the Lord showed me He always has my back in the midst of spiritual warfare.

DREAM

One night I dreamed that I was walking down the path of a dark road by myself. I was fearful because I sensed there was something behind me on this road. As I continued walking on the path, I felt whatever was there getting closer. I was afraid to turn around. In my spirit I sensed that it was a huge demonic entity. The evil presence drew closer.

Suddenly, just as I began to feel this malevolent being overtake me, I saw a gigantic lightning bolt strike the ground from the sky. I then heard an audible Voice that sounded like thunder say, "Leave him alone."

Immediately after I heard the Voice, the demonic presence that had been stalking me was suddenly sucked up into what felt like a giant vacuum cleaner. I turned around and I was alone on this road. I knew it was the voice of God the Father that I had heard.

INTERPRETATION

As you know by now, context is important to understanding the true meaning of our dreams. Before I had this particular dream, I was facing one of the most difficult challenges in my life. I was only in my early twenties at the time and still in the military. I was supposed to be headed to Germany to be stationed there for several years. As I prepared to leave from Fort Jackson, South Carolina, I became very ill and doctors discovered that I had an autoimmune disease affecting my kidneys. Instead of leaving for Germany, I was sent to a medical holding company in Fort Gordon, Georgia, to receive treatment.

The treatment was difficult. I had to receive a mild form of chemotherapy for several months and also prepare to face a medical review board that would decide if I was fit to stay in the military. In hindsight, the medical review really was the least of my worries. I wanted to know if I was going to be all right.

Though times were tough, I was grateful that the Lord placed a wonderful Christian couple in my life who supported me through this ordeal. We became good friends because we attended the same church back in South Carolina. Because I was stationed in Fort Gordon, Georgia, and awaiting my medical review, I would drive from Georgia every weekend to stay at their house in

South Carolina. They would take care of me as I recovered from nausea and weakness from the chemotherapy.

I would then make the two-hour ride with them back to our home church in McColl, South Carolina, on most weekends. They would drop me off at my parents' house and then they would stay the weekend with their family that lived only fifteen minutes away from my parents. On Sunday evening, they would pick me up and I would travel with them and their two small children back to Columbia in South Carolina, so I could rest before driving back to Fort Gordon for duty at 7:00 a.m.

You may wonder why I would include such a long explanation in interpreting a dream. I included my historical context because it is vital to understanding the magnitude of the dream. This was one of the most important dreams of my life, coming at a critical juncture when I needed assurance that I was going to be okay. The dream from the Holy Spirit gave me that assurance.

This was also the only time in my life when I heard the audible voice of God. The "dark road" in the dream made me think about what David wrote in Psalm 23: *"Yea, though I walk through the valley of the shadow of death, I will fear no evil; for You are with me; Your rod and Your staff, they comfort me"* (Psalm 23:4 NKJV).

PERMANENT ARSENAL

As I reflect on this dream almost thirty years later, I believe that the lightning served a twofold purpose. It reminded me of the awesome power of God, but was also a reminder of satan's expulsion from Heaven when Jesus said He saw him fall like lightning (Luke 10:18). These types of dreams are wonderful because they become a permanent part of your arsenal when engaging in spiritual warfare. The apostle Paul encouraged his spiritual son, Timothy, about the importance of using prophecy as a weapon:

> *So Timothy, my son, I am entrusting you with this responsibility, in keeping with the very first prophecies that were spoken over your life, and are now in the process of fulfillment in this great work of ministry, in keeping with the prophecies spoken over you. With this encouragement use your prophecies as weapons as you wage spiritual warfare by faith and with a clean conscience. For there are many who reject these virtues and are now destitute of the true faith* (1 Timothy 1:18-19 TPT).

Similar to personal prophecies spoken over our lives, dream encounters can serve the dreamer by revealing a prophetic picture that enables the dreamer to engage in spiritual warfare.

Oftentimes, Christians become disappointed with prophetic words that seemingly have fallen to the ground. They must war with the prophecies that were spoken over them by confessing those words aloud and staying in faith. The same is true with prophetic dreams. I often rehearse my dreams by reading my dream journal and confessing what the Lord has revealed to me. By practicing this exercise, I am encouraged and strengthened in my resolve that God will fulfill what He has shown me.

18

WHERE IS MY CAR?

Depending on the context, cars in dreams can be very symbolic. Similar to buses, cars can refer to your vocation or ministry. For instance, dreaming of being in a parked car and frustrated that you are not going anywhere may reveal you are discontented or stagnant in some area of your life or ministry. If you dream of being in a car, sitting in the passenger's seat with someone else driving, the Holy Spirit may be telling you that someone else is trying to control some aspect of your life, vocation, or ministry. Again, we must take into account the context of any automobile dream.

A TROUBLED PROPHET

Before going into detail about the next dream, I offer some context. There was a young prophet who was very gifted but had recently come under fire because it was alleged that he was plagiarizing the prophetic words he was releasing to people. This man had a national ministry and had grown quickly in popularity. It seemed as though he was being showcased on Christian television every other week. He even ministered to my wife and me at a conference we attended. As talk of alleged moral failure continued to surround his ministry, the Lord gave me a dream about him.

DREAM

In my dream I was driving my car. Suddenly the young minister who was surrounded by controversy was in a car ahead of me, which was off to the side of the road broken down. I decided to pull over on the other side of the street to see if I could help him. As I was helping him with his car, I suddenly looked over at my car across the street. To my utter shock, it was not there. In my haste to help the minister, someone had stolen my car. The dream ended with me looking for my car.

INTERPRETATION

Since we have already established that cars often refer to ministry, we can ascertain that the cars in this dream represent ministry. The broken-down car represents the ministry of the young minister who had been accused of falsifying prophetic words. He was under tremendous pressure to respond to the allegations surrounding his ministry. The car I was driving also represents ministry, as this man had ministered to me and my wife at a conference.

I was hesitant to receive the news about his misgivings in ministry due to having received what I believed to be accurate words from this person in the past. The fact that this minister's car was broken down on the side of the road represents the current condition of his ministry. In the dream, something was wrong with his car; and something was clearly wrong with this man's life and ministry.

My offer to help the man with his car in the dream signified my support of this person's ministry in the natural. I had been supportive of his ministry and had even defended him to others in the past. The dream served as a warning for me to keep my distance from his ministry. Why? Because in the dream, my car was actually stolen while helping him with his car.

STOLEN CARS AND A WORD OF WARNING

The stolen car in my dream was significant because car theft in dreams can represent stolen ministry.[1] It was not just any car, it was my car and my ministry at risk. The Lord was showing me that my association with this minister was dangerous. I heeded the warning that the

Lord gave me and this man was later exposed. Unfortunately, those who continued associating with him suffered tremendously in their personal lives due to his subsequent immorality.

I am so grateful for the Holy Spirit. I want to encourage you to heed the warnings and promptings of the Holy Spirit. Many years ago I learned a very important lesson about discernment from an older preacher. The preacher said, "Two plus two is four, not five." This was simple addition but the message he was conveying was that we should not give an extra point to someone just because we are familiar with them or are fond of them. We must trust our "gut" or discernment from the Holy Spirit in all matters.

In my case, I had received a dream about two cars. I could have disregarded this dream because I had positive interaction with the individual in my personal life and ministry. Perhaps the Lord has spoken to you in a similar way about someone. I encourage you to pay attention to what the Lord is revealing, even when you think you know someone. Do not give the extra point or the benefit of the doubt—always follow the Spirit's leading by searching out the truth no matter how difficult it may be to embrace.

As I conclude this section, I feel led to tell you about a mistake I made in regard to "giving the extra point" due to familiarity. The reason why I acted quickly in the case of the car dream was because of a painful memory associated with another minister I respected many years prior to this incident.

PAINFUL LESSON

One night I dreamed that a well-known minister of the gospel, whom I knew and supported financially, was being carried completely naked by another man on that man's shoulders. I was stunned by the vision but I began to let my reason get the best of me due to my love and admiration for this person. This minister had made a huge impact in my life and led me into the baptism of the Holy Spirit.

Instead of praying in response to the dream I had about him, I convinced myself that the dream was of the devil, because I didn't want to believe it. As time went on, I completely forgot about the dream until several weeks later when my wife broke the news to me that the minister had a short-term homosexual relationship with another minister on his church staff.

Needless to say, I was devastated by the news. How could this happen to such a spiritual giant in the faith? Although this person has since been restored, it was a painful experience for me. In hindsight, I do not believe it would have been as painful if I had not overlooked what the Lord was trying to show me in the night vision about the evangelist.

I want to encourage you to learn from my experience. Always follow the leading of the Holy Spirit. If the Lord reveals something unsuspected to you about someone, consider it an invitation to intercede. Pray for that person and ask the Holy Spirit to give you understanding about the dream. Remember that two plus two is four, not five. Don't give someone the extra point or overlook any warnings because of familiarity.

NOTE

1. Thompson and Beale, *The Divinity Code to Understanding Your Dreams and Visions*, Kindle.

19

SHE IS NOT A SERVANT

And which of you, having a servant plowing or tending sheep, will say to him when he has come in from the field, "Come at once and sit down to eat"? But will he not rather say to him, "Prepare something for my supper, and gird yourself and serve me till I have eaten and drunk, and afterward you will eat and drink"? Does he thank that servant because he did the things that were commanded him? I think not. So likewise you, when you have done all those things which you are commanded, say, "We are unprofitable servants. We have done what was our duty to do" (Luke 17:7-10 NKJV).

I believe the term slave or servant in Scripture does not get the attention it once did in our Christian circles because it conveys such a negative connotation, particularly among American Christians. We have been apprehensive at times to preach about true servanthood or associating ourselves with the notion of slavery in the Scriptures due to the concept of "wokeness"[1] in our current culture.

Even though we live in a racially charged, politically correct culture, we must still display courage by declaring the whole counsel of God. Servanthood is essential to the walk of the believer—it is an indicator of true Christianity. The words of Jesus in Matthew's gospel highlight the importance of this concept:

> But Jesus called them to Himself and said, "You know that the rulers of the Gentiles lord it over them, and those who are great exercise authority over them. Yet it shall not be so among you; but whoever desires to become great among you, let him be your servant. And whoever desires to be first among you, let him be your slave— just as the Son of Man did not come to be served, but to serve, and to give His life a ransom for many" (Matthew 20:25-28 NKJV).

The context of this passage in Matthew 20 reveals much about the significance of serving for the believer. Jesus' earthly life was about to come to an end. The mother of the sons of Zebedee asked Jesus to give her two sons a special place beside Him in His Kingdom in Heaven, that one son might sit to the right of Jesus and the other to the left. The disciples were indignant at the request that the sons should get special favor and then perhaps lord it over them. Jesus chose to use this incident to teach the disciples that the basis for relationship in the Kingdom is servanthood. (See Matthew 20:20-24.)

Jesus revealed to the disciples that the essence of His messianic mission was to serve and give His life for the world. Like Jesus, His disciples and all modern-day believers must embrace the role of the servant if they are to truly be like Christ. The apostle Paul even referred to himself as a "servant" as well as other ministry associates in most of his epistles (see Romans 1:1; Colossians 4:12; Philippians 1:1; 1 Timothy 4:6).

CONTEXT

Having established the importance of the concept of servanthood in the life of the believer, I would like to share a dream that I have titled, "She Is Not a Servant." The dream occurred several years ago when a young minister on my staff was considering marrying a young lady he was dating. At first my wife and I were delighted that the minister was dating this person. We were excited for the young man because we loved him and he was a son in the gospel.

Unfortunately, as he continued in the relationship, he began to have certain doubts about her walk with the Lord, and so did we. As the young man on my staff continued to date this woman and seek the Lord about the relationship, I had the following dream about them as a couple.

DREAM

In the dream I entered into a bedroom and saw the minister on my staff and the young woman he was considering marrying sitting together talking on the side of the bed. They did not know of my presence. It was as though I was invisible and was just there to observe the conversation. As I looked more closely into the face of the minister, I noticed that he was emotional and had tears in his eyes. As his girlfriend sat beside him, she said to him, "If you want it, it is going to cost you." After she made this statement, I heard another voice in the dream say the following words several times, "She's not a servant, she's not a servant, she's not a servant...."

INTERPRETATION

Because the minister on my staff was contemplating marriage with this woman, this dream was clearly a warning not to go through with it. The bedroom in the dream represents a place of intimacy for married couples. The woman in the dream told the minister that if he wanted it, it was going to "cost him." The young man was emotional with tears in eyes as he listened to her words. This signified that the relationship was going to cause him pain in the future. The voice that spoke in the dream that repeated the phrase, "She is not a servant" was an important part of the dream. I believe this was the voice of the Lord. This Voice is the reason why an understanding of servanthood in Scripture is so essential.

As previously mentioned, servanthood was central to the mission of Jesus and is also paramount to the life of any believer. It is recorded in Matthew's gospel in the parable of the talents that the Lord will say to those entering Heaven the following, *"His lord said to him, 'Well done, good and faithful servant; you were faithful over a few things, I will make you ruler over many things. Enter into the joy of your lord'"* (Matthew 25:21 NKJV). Paul, in Romans 6:15-16, also gives insight into the concept of servanthood by encouraging believers to be slaves of righteousness and not slaves of sin leading to death.

The fact that the Lord was emphatically saying to me in the dream that this young woman was not a servant was a serious red flag. It went to the heart of her current walk with the Lord.

How Was I to Respond

How was I to respond? I wanted the best for my spiritual son in the gospel but I also knew that I was treading into some sensitive territory. This was the woman he loved and I didn't want to drop a bomb like this on him because it could have led to a rift between the two of us at the time.

In prayer, I asked the Lord for wisdom. The Holy Spirit spoke and led me into a fast for several weeks about the situation.

Before I continue with this story, I want to interrupt here to give you some advice as to how to respond should the Holy Spirit reveal potentially life-changing information to you about someone you love in this kind of dilemma.

First and foremost, make it your priority to pray for the person and ask God for wisdom. If the person is in this serious kind of relationship, you can't just share your dream and expect them to drop everything. You must bathe the situation in prayer. From experience, in my haste and immaturity as a young dreamer, I shared prophetic dreams with people about individuals they loved and admired without waiting on the Lord. Needless to say, my sharing was not well taken because the person was not ready to receive the information. Oftentimes, they were too emotionally attached and instead of helping the situation, it backfired.

Second, as you pray for the person, be patient and know that God loves them more than you do. The Lord is already working on their hearts in some way. He gave you the dream to co-labor with Him in bringing this person to the point of making the right decision.

Third, follow the Lord's leading about what you should actually do in every situation. In prayer, did the Lord give you an instruction to follow? Does He want you to add fasting to your prayers? Does He want you to eventually tell the person the dream after soaking it in prayer, or does He just want you to keep interceding without ever revealing what you know? Whatever He tells you to do, be obedient! God gave you the dream because He wants to use you.

Let's get back to our story. How did our story end? After prayer and asking the Lord for wisdom, the Holy Spirit led me to fast for several weeks for the young minister. The Lord informed me that I was to meet with him for dinner after my time of fasting was over. I was actually pretty nervous because I knew the risk associated with sharing this kind of dream with a man considering marriage. If his heart was not ready, our relationship would suffer because *an offended friend is harder to win back than a fortified city* (Proverbs 18:19 NLT).

As I shared the dream, however, I sensed God's grace on me. The Holy Spirit had already been working on his heart. The dream I shared served as confirmation for him and gave him the confidence to end the relationship. He actually did not have peace about proceeding with the relationship, and he confirmed my dream about the character issues in this woman's life. This man today is happily married to a lovely woman and they have three beautiful children.

Because I considered the Lord and responded as He led me, my friend was able to hear my concerns. The Lord had prepared his heart during those weeks of fasting and prayer.

NOTE

1. www.dictionary.Cambridge.org

20

WORK ON YOUR CHARACTER

The Holy Spirit will sometimes give us dreams about people who were dear to us who are deceased. I have stated how the Lord provided healing for me after my brother's death by allowing me to see him one more time in a dream about Heaven. These dreams provide emotional healing and give us closure. A vision may also include one final message from the person that the Lord wants you to adopt in your life or ministry.

On February 15, 2015, John Paul Jackson, founder of Streams Ministries, passed away due to complications with an aggressive form of cancer. He was a father in the faith to many and was recognized as the authority on biblical dream interpretation for more than thirty years. Though I had never met Jackson in person, I was mentored by him in dreams and interpretation. After hearing of his death, I was saddened because he had played such a big part in helping me understand my gifting in the seer realm. I had a dream about him the following evening.

DREAM

In my dream I saw recently deceased John Paul Jackson. He looked into my eyes and said the following words, "Work on your character." The dream ended right after he finished speaking.

INTERPRETATION

This dream was basically one final word of exhortation from my mentor. Though I never met John Paul Jackson in person, we were connected in the spirit because I spent so much time learning from him. The message, "Work on your character" was important for three reasons. The first reason is that Jackson was known by those close to him to promote character over giftedness. John's close friend and ministry associate R.T. Kendall shared the following comments at Jackson's memorial service:

> I spent about thirty minutes making a video for use at his memorial service. Because of time it was edited down to seven or eight minutes. One of the things left out (they had to edit it because of time for other speakers) was John

Paul's emphasis on "character is more important than gifting." One would have thought
this goes without saying, but, sadly, there were
a surprising number of Charismatic leaders
who opposed this teaching. John Paul's view
regarding character over gifting was one of the
main things that made me feel comfortable
about him. Holiness is more important than
seeing miracles.[1]

After the dream and upon learning that character was
John Paul Jackson's life message, my faith was stirred up
on the inside. I was greatly encouraged that the Lord gave
me the dream.

The second reason why the message about character
from the dream is important is because the vision served
as a constant reminder to do everything with integrity in
my life and ministry. It also reminds me that I am a work
in progress and the Lord is continuing to mold me into
the person He wants me to be.

Third, I believe the message John Paul Jackson gave
in the dream about character was a general word for the
larger Body of Christ, particularly those who operate in
church ministry. If the Body of Messiah is going to be
effective in reaching the world with the gospel, we must
operate in His character. As I conclude this chapter, I am
reminded of the words of Paul:

And not only that, but we also glory in trib-ulations, knowing that tribulation produces perseverance; and perseverance, character; and character, hope (Romans 5:3-4 NKJV).

NOTE

1. R.T. Kendall, "John Paul Jackson (1950-2015)," https://rtkendallministries.com/john-paul-jackson-1950-2015; accessed September 18, 2021.

21

THE COUNTERFEIT

How do tellers at banks know when they have encountered a counterfeit bill? There are actually several ways in which banks check to see if the cash they receive is genuine. First, they can process large amounts of cash through a cash counter machine. If there is a counterfeit bill, it will be rejected by the machine. Another way to identify counterfeit money is that the images on it may look blurry. Though I could mention other ways banks use to identify the counterfeit, the principal method tellers use to determine whether a bill is counterfeit is their training to identify real money.

In essence, after handling thousands of dollars of cash every day, they know how the genuine bills feel to their touch. Because they handle real money so often, they can easily identify the counterfeit because it doesn't feel the same as the real.

Similarly, in this book I have focused on real spiritual dreams that the Holy Spirit has given me through the years. You have read a variety of ways the Lord communicates in dreams. There have been dreams that warn, encourage, heal, and prophesy. I pray that through reading about my dreams, you will become like a bank teller. Since you have focused on the genuine, you are now ready to discern the counterfeit dreams.

Satan the Counterfeiter

Though we live in a world with real evil, behind that evil we must understand that we are actually wrestling with a real devil (Ephesians 6:12). Satan is called the prince of the power of the air (Ephesians 2:2). He is also known as the god of this world who blinds people to the truth of the glorious gospel of Jesus Christ (2 Corinthians 4:4).

One of the ways satan blinds people is through deception and counterfeit spirituality. God is the Creator and satan is the great counterfeiter. In his second letter to the Corinthians, the apostle Paul warned against false apostles who had embraced the ways of the devil through counterfeit spirituality.

But what I do, I will also continue to do, that I may cut off the opportunity from those who desire an opportunity to be regarded just as we are in the things of which they boast. For such are false apostles, deceitful workers, transforming themselves into apostles of Christ. And no wonder! For Satan himself transforms himself into an angel of light. Therefore it is no great thing if his ministers also transform themselves into ministers of righteousness, whose end will be according to their works (2 Corinthians 11:12-15 NKJV).

Jesus our Lord also warned that the last days would be marked by counterfeit christs, false prophets, and lying signs and wonders (Matthew 24:24; Mark 13:22). One way the enemy deceives is through counterfeit dreams and visions.

DEFINING THE COUNTERFEIT DREAM

In her book *Dreams and Visions: Understanding and Interpreting God's Messages to You,* Jane Hamon describes the essence of the false dream: "A false dream or vision is one that attempts to establish ungodly principles or deception concerning biblical truth in the mind of the dreamer or in those to whom the dreamer tells the dream."[1]

In essence, the false dream has the same purpose as the false prophet.[2] The end result is to lead people away from God and toward the enemy. The book of Deuteronomy gives us more insight about the serious nature of spurious dreams.

> *If there arises among you a prophet or a dreamer of dreams, and he gives you a sign or a wonder, and the sign or the wonder comes to pass, of which he spoke to you, saying, "Let us go after other gods"—which you have not known— "and let us serve them," you shall not listen to the words of that prophet or that dreamer of dreams, for the Lord your God is testing you to know whether you love the Lord your God with all your heart and with all your soul. You shall walk after the Lord your God and fear Him, and keep His commandments and obey His voice; you shall serve Him and hold fast to Him. But that prophet or that dreamer of dreams shall be put to death, because he has spoken in order to turn you away from the Lord your God, who brought you out of the land of Egypt and redeemed you from the house of bondage, to entice you from the way in which the Lord your God commanded you to walk. So you shall put away the evil from your midst (Deuteronomy 13:1-5 NKJV).*

Though we are no longer required by the Lord to put false prophets and false dreamers to death, we must understand that there are still serious consequences for those who abandon the truth of the Word of God and align themselves with those who claim revelation that does not line up with Scripture.

A good example of this kind of deception is found in the origins of the religion of Islam. Many are unaware that the Islamic leader Muhammad claimed that he had prophetic visions in which the angel "Gabriel" came to give him new revelation. In fact, Islam's holy book, the Quran, is a compilation of "prophetic visions" given to Muhammad to bring a new gospel and a new way to please Allah, whom Muslims worship as God.

Another example is found in the history of the Mormon church with its founder Joseph Smith.

In 1823 in Western New York, Smith claimed that he had a vision in which an angel named "Moroni" told him about engraved golden plates buried on a hill named Cumorah (also known as Mormon Hill). According to Smith, he received subsequent revelations from Moroni and was later able to excavate the plates, translating them into English. From the translated golden plates, Smith produced the Book of Mormon. The Book of Mormon, according to Smith, was named after an ancient American prophet who originally compiled the text recorded on the plates. The text from the plates supposedly recounts the history of a family of Israelites that migrated to America centuries before Jesus Christ. The text claims that these people were taught by prophets similar to those in the Old Testament. In essence, the Book of Mormon written by Joseph Smith was another gospel.

Whether it was the angel "Gabriel" or the angel "Moroni," the visions that Muhammad and Joseph Smith claimed to have had directly conflicts with Scripture. The apostle Paul wrote the following warning to the Galatians:

> *I marvel that you are turning away so soon from Him who called you in the grace of Christ, to a different gospel, which is not another; but there are some who trouble you and want to pervert the gospel of Christ. But even if we, or an angel from heaven, preach any other gospel ,to you than what we have preached to you, let him be accursed. As we have said before, so now I say again, if anyone preaches any other gospel to you than what you have received, let him be accursed* (Galatians 1:6-9 NKJV).

If Paul's warning was adhered to by both men—Muhammad and Joseph Smith—one has to question what the landscape of religion would look like today.

As stated previously, dreamers and visionaries can avoid similar pitfalls if they compare every dream, vision, and revelation with what is written in Scripture. Although God does lead us through dreams at times, we must never substitute supernatural experiences—dreams, visions, personal prophecies, etc.—for the study of His Word or the leading of the Holy Spirit and prayer. Dreams should serve as confirmation of the experiences.

EXAMPLES OF COUNTERFEIT DREAMS

Nightmares

What about nightmares? Let me first say that not every nightmare is from the enemy. God can also use an unpleasant dream to get our attention. As mentioned earlier, King Abimelech had a scary dream from the Lord that he was a *"dead man"* for taking the wife of Abraham into his harem (Genesis 20:3). Pilate's wife also had a nightmare about Jesus, claiming that she had *"suffered many things"* about Jesus in her dream (Matthew 27:19).

Sometimes prophetic dreams and visions may resemble nightmares. The prophet Daniel also experienced this kind of terror as he was resting on his bed in Babylon when he saw four great beasts coming out of the sea (Daniel 7:1-8). Daniel admitted that he was actually grieved in his spirit by the night visions and that he was actually troubled by them similar to Pilate's wife concerning Jesus. Daniel's "nightmares" actually turned out to be prophetic insights about future kingdoms that would arise on earth (see Daniel 7:1-28).

For instance, many Christians testify to having dreams of being chased by someone and being terrified. Dreams like these are not always demonically inspired. The Lord could be giving you the dream to expose fear in your life. It could be a dream about your own condition. For example, a dream could be given to show dreamers that they are running away from their responsibilities. I have had dreams like this and have actually "turned the tables" on the person pursuing me by chasing my pursuer. God wants us to get to the point where we as believers never back down—rather, we are led by His Spirit.

Nightmares can also serve as a signal that the dreamer is carrying around unresolved issues in their soul (mind, will, and emotions). Or the Lord may be allowing us to dream about a traumatic experience buried deeply in our subconscious. If as a believer you are having constant nightmares, please see a Christian, Spirit-filled counselor or deliverance minister. We are called as believers to bear one another's burdens. Never be ashamed to ask for help.

If satan can give false visions to people and start world religions, then he has no problem manipulating what we see in our sleep at night or deceiving us or filling us with fear. The devil was able to show Jesus all the kingdoms of the world and their glory (Matthew 4:8). Most Bible scholars believe that the devil showed Jesus these kingdoms in a supernatural vision.

Some nightmares occur because we have actually allowed the enemy to gain a foothold through our physical senses. For instance, some believers love to watch explicit films loaded with violence, fear, and sexuality. They don't realize, however, that these "entertaining" films attract demonic spirits to them. Viewing a violent scene in a movie that shows a person being murdered by a psychopath is not a good idea just before bedtime. You may attract spirits of hate, murder, and fear leading to a demonically inspired nightmare where you dream of some evil person attacking you with a machete.

Our spiritual senses not only refer to the eyes but also the ears. Over twenty-plus years ago, while teaching at a Christian high school, I decided to perform a little experiment with one of my students. I had several students in my class who loved to listen to hip-hop music.

Let me just say from the outset that this is not a diatribe about this form of music. There are some great artists out there who have a positive message. However on this particular day, I wanted to teach one of my students a lesson as I prepared to teach my 12th-grade Bible class.

Oftentimes, students would walk into class with their headphones on, which was actually against the rules. On this particular day, I asked one of my students what he was listening to. He responded that I would not approve of his selection. I knew it was loaded with vulgarity.

On most days I would just tell him to take off the headset and prepare for class. But this day, I tried something different. I told him to keep his headphones on and play his music. Then I placed a Bible in his hand. I asked him to turn to the book of Philippians and asked him to read the following verse while simultaneously listening to the music:

> *Finally, brethren, whatever things are true, whatever things are noble, whatever things are just, whatever things are pure, whatever things are lovely, whatever things are of good report, if there is any virtue and if there is anything praiseworthy—meditate on these things* (Philippians 4:8 NKJV).

As the young man tried to listen to his music while reading the Philippians passage, he started to shake his head and took off his headphones.

"What's wrong?" I asked.

He said, "It don't fit."

Those three simple words from this young man on that day still speak volumes to me. What we listen to can have a profound effect on our spiritual walk and our dream lives. The enemy can torment us as we sleep by what we *hear* as well as what we *see*. We must close *all* doors to the enemy. The images and sounds we as believers are allowing to defile our hearts and minds do not "fit" with people who are supposed to be moving toward godliness (see 1 Timothy 4:7).

DECEPTIVE DREAMS

When people think of the devil, images sometimes come to mind of a red guy with horns, a bifurcated tail, and a pitchfork. This, however, is not how the Bible describes satan. The Bible describes him as an *"angel of light"* (2 Corinthians 11:14). He comes to deceive us as someone that seems harmless. I have already mentioned how the enemy will give dreams and visions from "angels" to give counterfeit revelation.

An interesting example of satan's treacherous nature is found in the book of Jeremiah where the prophet writes a letter to the exiles, informing them that they were to prepare to be in Babylon for seventy years. Jeremiah's prophecy contradicted the false prophets who were preparing the Jews for a short stay in Babylon and a quick return to their homeland in Jerusalem.

This is what the Lord of Heaven's Armies, the God of Israel, says to all the captives he has exiled to Babylon from Jerusalem: "Build homes, and plan to stay. Plant gardens, and eat the food they produce. Marry and have children. Then find spouses for them so that you may have many grandchildren. Multiply! Do not dwindle away! And work for the peace and prosperity of the city where I sent you into exile. Pray to the Lord for it, for its welfare will determine your welfare."

This is what the Lord of Heaven's Armies, the God of Israel, says: "Do not let your prophets and fortune-tellers who are with you in the land of Babylon trick you. Do not listen to their dreams, because they are telling you lies in my name. I have not sent them," says the Lord (Jeremiah 29:4-9 NLT).

An important aspect of Jeremiah's prophecy is the warning he gave in verse 8: *"Do not let your prophets and your diviners deceive you, nor listen to your dreams which you cause to be dreamed."* In essence, the perversity and disobedience of the people of Judah caused the false prophets to have false dreams. Because their hearts were not right before God, the people's own sinful ways brought more deception. The result was tragic, especially for those who prophesied falsely and for the people who were led into deeper deception (Jeremiah 28:15-17; 29:15-32). Though his name was not mentioned in the story of Jeremiah, satan was the cause of the false dreams and lies from the false prophets.

A Word of Warning for Today

I believe the example included from the book of Jeremiah is relevant for today. The reason why the people could not discern the truth from Jeremiah compared to the false prophets was because they had not repented of their sins. The people actually made the false prophets tell them what they wanted to hear. It is easy to be deceived when we are not putting God's Word into action in our lives. In the New Testament, the book of James warns us of the consequences of not living by the Word of God:

> *But be doers of the word, and not hearers only, deceiving yourselves. For if anyone is a hearer of the word and not a doer, he is like a man observing his natural face in a mirror; for he observes himself, goes away, and immediately forgets what kind of man he was. But he who looks into the perfect law of liberty and continues in it, and is not a forgetful hearer but a doer of the work,*

this one will be blessed in what he does (James 1:22-25 NKJV).

We have a choice to be "doers" of the Word of God or "forgetful hearers." You will not be deceived by a false prophet or false dream if you make it your priority to obey God's Word in every circumstance. As you make this commitment, you will avoid getting an appetite for what Timothy describes as "itching ears" for false teachers with deceptive dreams (2 Timothy 4:3-4).

DARK, DISCOURAGING DREAMS

I have debated myself as to what to label dreams from the enemy that make us wake up feeling like we have no hope. Some people label these dreams as dark or discouraging dreams. In his book *Decoding Your Spiritual Dreams: Keys for Christian Dream Interpretation,* Bryan Carraway provides helpful insights on satan's purpose for dark dreams and also teaches dreamers how to discern a dark dream from a God-inspired spiritual dream:

> Satan has many purposes for dark dreams. He sends them primarily to torment, confuse, and deceive. The forces of the dark kingdom can send dreams to both Christians and non-Christians.... Dreams from the enemy are always dark or deceptive in some way. Many

people report that dreams from the enemy come in darker, muted colors, or entirely in black and white. Dark dreams usually leave one with no hope, no way of escape, and amidst the depressing themes, there seems to be no positive aspect at all—no offer of redemption. Dreams from the Lord don't have that quality. Spiritual dreams can sometimes deal with very dark themes (spiritual warfare, the tactics of the enemy, divine judgment, etc.) but, in spiritual dreams, there is a redeeming message or some avenue of hope portrayed in the dream. God is a God of mercy, and even in harsh spiritual dreams, we see His divine attributes of grace, mercy, or love contained somewhere within.[3]

I mentioned previously that my older brother was murdered when he was only twenty years old.

After some time had passed, I also shared that God gave me a wonderful healing dream about speaking with my brother in Heaven. I woke up feeling encouraged and experienced a real sense of closure. Shortly after having this healing dream however, the enemy gave me a counterfeit dream to try and discourage me. The dream follows.

DREAM

In my dream I saw my older brother in a dark place. He looked very tired and sad. The atmosphere in the dream was depressing with no hope, without words being spoken.

As previously mentioned, dreams sent from the enemy are usually darker in appearance, devoid of hope and simply depressing. Such was the case with this dream. When I woke from the dream, fear, sadness, and confusion surrounded me. As I compared this dark dream with the one about my brother in Heaven, I became convinced that the enemy had sent this dream to discourage me.

Satan wanted to break the peace and momentum I had gained from seeing the earlier vision of my brother. The enemy wanted me to start doubting what I was shown from the Lord. He wanted to stop me from sharing my testimony and encouraging other people, especially those in my family.

UNDERSTANDING THE NATURE OF GOD

Another way to have confidence in deciphering the counterfeit dream is to have a clear understanding of the nature of God. The Bible declares that God is not the author of confusion; rather, He brings peace

(1 Corinthians 14:33). Through the dream, the enemy tried to bring confusion about the whereabouts of my brother. God would never bring confusion, especially after encouraging me and giving me so much clarity in the previous dream.

The dream also brought fear. Though warning dreams from the Lord can put the fear of God into us, lead us into spiritual warfare, or cause us to walk in holiness, satan sends dreams to torment us with fear. It is in God's nature to love. In fact, God is love and mature love will eradicate fear (1 John 4:7-18). When the Lord sends a dream with dark themes, it is still motivated by love.

Last, God is a redemptive God! He sent His only begotten Son to redeem us because we were lost. Satanic dreams, like the one I had about my brother, have no redemptive elements in them. In these kinds of dreams, there is usually no hope and no way out of the misery. Even in the Old Testament as a prophetic utterance came forth promising destructive consequences because of sin, God always gave a redemptive message of hope if the people would obey His commands.

CLOSING ADVICE ABOUT THE COUNTERFEIT

Some people in the Body of Christ spend most of their time focusing on the counterfeit. Unfortunately, in their efforts to discern the false prophets, false words, or false dreams, they have not spent enough time familiarizing themselves with the genuine. Like tellers at banks, we can discern the fake if we spend most of our time with the genuine. Jesus said, *"My sheep hear My voice, and I know them, and they follow Me"* (John 10:27 NKJV). If we spend enough time in the presence of God and in His Word, we will get to know the nature of God better. We will also be able to hear His voice in our dreams and have our senses developed to the point where we can discern good from evil (Hebrews 5:14).

NOTES

1. Jane Hamon, *Dreams and Visions: Understanding and Interpreting God's Messages to You* (Chosen Books, 2016), Kindle Edition, 35.
2. Ibid.
3. Bryan Carraway, *Decoding Your Spiritual Dreams: Keys for Christian Dream Interpretation* (Maitland, FL: Xulon Press, 2017), 68-69.

22

FIREBALLS FROM JESUS AND THE CONCLUSION

As you know by now, dream encounters have the ability to transform our lives in such a way that we are never the same. Some of these experiences are so vivid that when you wake from them you can't determine whether you actually traveled to another realm or not. Such was the case when I was in my early twenties, almost thirty years ago. I had a dream encounter with the Lord Jesus that I treasure and hold dear to my heart every day. I also consider it to be the most impactful dream I ever had.

DREAM

In my dream, I am in Heaven and lying down on what appeared to be an altar. All of a sudden, I see Jesus above me, looking down at me smiling as I am lying on my back. He then begins to toss fireballs down to me over His shoulder. The fireballs go right to the center of my being. The fireballs do not hurt, they feel wonderful. The feeling is really indescribable. The only phrase that comes close is total ecstasy. Jesus continued smiling and throwing down fireballs until He reached the number seven and then stopped. I didn't want it to stop. I wanted more. Shortly after He stopped the flow of fireballs, I woke up from the dream.

INTERPRETATION

And from the throne proceeded lightnings, thunderings, and voices. Seven lamps of fire were burning before the throne, which are the seven Spirits of God (Revelation 4:5 NKJV).

Most Bible scholars agree that the seven Spirits of God actually refer to the Holy Spirit. The Lord showed me that the seven fireballs represented the fullness of the Holy Spirit. Seven is a number of fullness or completion. According to the gospel of John, Jesus is the Baptizer in the Holy Spirit (John 1:33). The tossing of the seven fireballs signified the Lord baptizing me in the Holy Spirit. Glory to God!

Although I am grateful for every supernatural encounter the Lord gives me, this is the one that I meditate on when times get tough. I am reminded that I am not alone and that Jesus has baptized me with the precious gift of the Holy Spirit. This dream propelled me into ministry as well. I knew that Jesus had set me apart for Himself and was calling me to walk in the Spirit.

Last, the encounter created a hunger for me to experience more of God. Though I didn't have full comprehension at the time of the encounter with the Lord, this experience set me on a quest to know Him and make Him known to others.

CONCLUSION

I chose to conclude with the fireball dream for two reasons. First, the dream impacted me more than any dream I ever had. It serves today as a springboard for everything I do in ministry.

Second, I believe the dream sums up the true purpose for all supernatural dream encounters from the Lord—intimacy with God. Genuine, supernatural dream encounters should always draw us closer to Jesus.

If my personal dream journey has made you want to dream more, understand your dreams, increase your desire to help others interpret their dreams, and make you want more intimacy with the Lord, then I have achieved my goal in writing this book!

APPENDIX A

GLOSSARY OF COMMON DREAM SYMBOLS (ABRIDGED)

The following glossary has been adapted from several sources: Bryan Carraway's *Decoding Your Spiritual Dreams: Keys for Christian Dream interpretation* (Xulon Press, 2017), 98-131; Adam F. Thompson and Adrian Beale's *The Divinity Code to Understanding Your Dreams and Visions* (Destiny Image Publishers, 2011), 219-594; www.unlockingyourdreams.org; and my personal experience as a seer. For a more thorough treatment of dream symbols, please refer to these sources.

A

Airplane—(size and type of plane correlates to the interpretation) prophetic ministry; going to heights in the Spirit; new and higher understanding

Alligator (Crocodile)—ancient evil; hidden danger, upcoming verbal attack orchestrated by the enemy, evil in the past, demon

Attic—history; past issues; family history; spiritual realm

B

Baby—new ministry or responsibility that has recently been birthed; new beginning; new idea; dependent, helpless; innocent; sin

Basement—hidden; forgotten; hidden issues; foundation; basics

Bathroom—spiritual cleansing, deliverance; secret lust (sin); refreshing

Bathroom in full view—humbling season; others aware of cleansing; transparency

Bear—enemy; stealer of young Christians; powerful spiritual force; economic loss (as in "a bear market"); Russia

Bed—God (as the place of our rest) rest; sex; intimacy; adultery, laziness

Bed (Under Bed)—hidden; secret; cover up; foundation

Bedroom—private; intimacy or union; inner circle (confide in); the place of heart communion, covenant (as in marriage)

Bee/Hornet—painful; strong, demonic attack

Bicycle—individual ministry or calling requiring perseverance; individual on a humbling journey (no horsepower); self-propelled ministry (doing things in your own strength)

Black—death, mystery; sin, deceitful; famine; financially sound (depending on context as in the "black")

Blue—revelation, communion; Holy Spirit

Bus—church or ministry; transition in vocation, ministry or life

C

Car—how well (or not) a person is progressing through life; one's ministry or ministry gift; vocation or job

Cat—self-willed; untrainable; predator; unclean spirit; bewitching charm; stealthy, sneaky, or deceptive; something precious in the context of a personal pet

Cow—subsistence; prosperity

D

Dog—friend; unbeliever/fool; an attitude that rejects God's authority; symbolizes the world; the flesh; someone who turns on you; religious hypocrites

E

Eagle—prophetic; prophetic calling; prophet (seer); God; strength

Elevator—(ascending) spiritual or natural promotion; (descending) spiritual or natural progress that is being hindered in some way

F

Fish—believers; human souls

Flying—call or ability to move in the higher things of God; understanding the spirit realm of God; the current level of mastery or victory attained in relation to some issue or season of life

G

Gold—refined/pure/holy; glory; wealthy, great, or powerful; anointing

Grapes—good fruit; blood; sacrifice (crushed); fruitfulness; success in life

Grasshopper—destruction; drought, pestilence

H

Horse—power, strength, conquest; spiritual warfare

House—a person, their life, their spiritual state; the present condition of one's life; ministry; church

K

Kitchen—heart (as in the "kitchen is the heart of the home"); spiritual preparation; going deep in the Word; spiritual food & feasting; under pressure (as in turning up the heat)

L

Library—learning; knowledge; research

Lion—symbolizes authority (king); Jesus Christ; the devil; royalty, kingship, bravery

M-N

Mountain—spiritual high place; heaven; impossibility; obstacle; place of encountering God

Nakedness—being transparent; humility; innocence (in a positive sense); lust; temptation; in or of the flesh (in a negative sense)

Nose—discernment, led

O

Ocean Liner—impacting large numbers of people

Octopus—Jezebel spirit because of the tentacles; fleshly control or influence (tentacles); controlling spirit; soul-tie stronghold (octopus on head)

Onion(s)—represents the world (Egypt); dwelling in the past and getting upset over nothing (tears from peeling onions); focusing on the past, having murky vision

P

Pig—unbeliever; sin; unclean spirit; devil/demon; gluttonous; vicious, vengeful

Police Officer—authority for good or evil; protector; spiritual authority; angels

Purple—authority, royalty; false authority (negative)

R

Rain—blessing; cleansing; favor of God, spiritual outpouring (revival); trouble from enemy (dirty rain)

Rat—feeds on garbage or impurities; unclean spirit, invader

Red—wisdom, anointing, power; anger; war

Roller Coaster—a wild ride that God is directing, exciting, but temporary; a path of destruction that first appears exciting; an emotionally trying time with ups and downs

Roof—spiritual covering; protection

S

School/Classroom—training period; a place of teaching; teaching ministry; teaching anointing; discipleship

Scorpion—demonic power; stinging words; torment; betrayal; evil spirits; evil men

Sheep—believers; Christ; sinners (lost or astray); Church (flock of sheep); vulnerable; humility; submission; sacrifice

Shepherd—Christ; God; pastor; hireling; greedy pastors; false shepherds; protector

Shield—faith; protection; God's truth; faith in God

Sword—Word of God; far reaching; authority

Shoes—Gospel of peace; preparation; ministry

Silver—redemption, grace; wealth, treasure

Snake—deception, lies; satan; unforgiveness, bitterness; deceptive person pretending to be righteous/false prophet (white snake); evil spirit

Snow—blessing; refreshing; righteousness; purity; grace

Spider—occult attack; witchcraft; issue or stronghold; an issue that raises fear or has the potential to be messy to deal with; threat (with a danger of entanglement)

Staircase—up: promotion; down: demotion, backsliding, failure; heavenly portal; up or down in the spirit and anointing; steps that need to be taken

Storms—disturbance; change; spiritual warfare; judgment; sudden calamity or destruction; turbulent times; trial; opposition

Submarine—not openly shown or not public; underground church; church in the Spirit; spiritual vessel not yet revealed; the Spirit (submarine searching underwater)

Subway—undercover and active, but not seen by many; a behind the scenes ministry, hidden ministry

Swimming Pool—place of spiritual refreshing; a place of God's Spirit; immersed in God; dirty water can indicate spiritual pollution, corruption or backslidden condition; ready for baptism

T

Teeth—wisdom; comprehension; understanding

Teeth Falling Out—loss of wisdom; loss of power; losing face; shame

Tent—human body; temporary church; earthly dwelling place (contrasted with heavenly home); meeting place with God

Theater—on display, visible; going to be shown something; clarity; spiritual sight; fleshly lust

Tiger—strong evil force; satan; vicious religious spirit; danger; powerful minister (both good and evil), soul power

Tornadoes—destruction, danger; judgment; drastic change; winds of change (negative or positive depending on the color of the tornadoes); the devil; judgment against sin; unstoppable; trials and calamity; spirit of death

Train—a movement of God; denomination; large (continuous) ministry; vehicle to destiny; the Church

Trees—person; righteous believer; Jesus Christ; country or nation; the cross; leaders; mature believers; steady

U-V

Umbrella—covering; protection; authority structure; shield

Vulture—scavenger; unclean; impure; an evil person; greedy

W

Water—Holy Spirit; refreshing; Word of God; spiritual life; the blessing of God

Whale—big impact in the things of the Spirit; going deep in the spirit; prophetic ministry (leader who is sensitive to the Spirit); influential believer

White—righteousness, holiness; religious spirit (negative), legalistic

Wind—change (as in "winds of change are blowing"); Holy Spirit

Window—prophetic gifting (seeing through window); entrance to the soul; insight/revelation; opportunity (as in an "open window of opportunity")

Wine—Holy Spirit; joy; communion; resurrection; prosperity/plenty; drunkenness; love of the world

Wolf—satan; unregenerate predators; predatory ministers; false prophets; those who ruthlessly destroy people for selfish gain

Z

Zoo— strange; chaos; commotion; very busy place; noisy strife

NUMBERS

1—God; singular; unity

2—multiplication; confirmation; division, separation

3—the Trinity, God

4—God's creative works

5—grace, redemption; protection; deliverance

6—humankind; human effort; carnality

7—perfection, completion

8—new beginnings; new cycle or new era; eternality

9—judgment; fruitfulness; fullness of the Spirit; end or conclusion

10—completeness; full

11—disorder; disintegration ; imperfection /incompleteness; transition

12—divine government; apostolic fullness

13—rebellion; apostasy; corruption; backsliding

30—begin ministry

40—period of trial/testing/probation/proving which closes in victory or discipline

50—Jubilee; liberty/liberation; release/freedom; deliverance/rest; Pentecost; the perfect consummation of time; extreme grace

APPENDIX B

Practical Advice for Dreamers

Though we have covered much ground in the area of dreams and interpretation, I now give you some practical advice so you can thrive in this mysterious world of dreams. The following guidance will help you maximize your dream life to the fullest.

Get a Good Night's Sleep Regularly

I understand that there are times because of our busy schedules that we might need to stay up later than usual. You must understand, however, that going to bed too late can affect your dream life. The human body has two distinct modes of sleep—REM sleep and NREM sleep. REM (rapid eye movement) is the deep sleep cycle and the cycle for dreaming. During REM sleep, our eyes move around rapidly in a range of directions but do not send any visual information to your brain. NREM (non-rapid eye movement) sleep has three stages. In order to get to REM sleep, you have to first go through the three stages of NREM sleep. The first two stages of NREM sleep are considered light sleep, preparing us for deep sleep. If we always go to bed late, we will have limited time in REM sleep and our dream lives will be hindered merely from a physiological standpoint. Besides, getting between 7-8 hours every night provides needed rest for your own good health and well-being.

SUBMIT YOUR SLEEP TO GOD

Before I go to bed every night, I say a prayer and submit my sleep to the Lord. I consecrate my dream life to the Lord. Sleeping is a holy thing in the Fox household. If we commit our day to the Lord when we awake in the morning, we should also commit our sleep to Him every night. Part of committing my sleep to the Lord is asking God to reveal Himself to me in dreams and to give me revelation. You can do the same thing. I am reminded of Luke 12:32 (NKJV): *"Do not fear, little flock, for it is your Father's good pleasure to give you the kingdom."* It is the Father's good pleasure to reveal Himself to you.

SET THE RIGHT ATMOSPHERE BEFOREHAND

Setting the right spiritual atmosphere is important for your dream life. You will be more susceptible to having a spiritual dream from the Lord if you engage in the right activities before going to bed for the evening. The following are part of my pre-sleep routine.

RESEARCH BOOKS AND ONLINE CHRISTIAN MATERIAL ABOUT DREAMS AND VISIONS

Reading or viewing online Christian material about the subject of dreams and visions before turning in for the evening can build up your spiritual hunger and even enable you to receive an impartation before retiring for the evening. I have experienced this many times. I began to notice that my dreams increased after watching online videos from the late seer prophet John Paul Jackson. As I continued to watch the online videos, I became hungrier for the Lord. I began to read and study more about dreams.

Even right now as you read this book, you are setting the right atmosphere for a spiritual dream encounter because of the hunger you are developing in your heart for the Lord and for the mysteries He wants to reveal to you in the night season of rest. No matter how much

I dream, I still make it a practice to read and watch anointed people before going to sleep for the evening.

AVOID WATCHING OR READING THE NEWS BEFORE BEDTIME

Watching the late news on television or even reading news on your phone or the Internet before heading off to sleep can have an adverse effect on your dream life. The book of Isaiah declares the following: *"For behold, the darkness shall cover the earth, and deep darkness the people; but the Lord will arise over you, and His glory will be seen upon you"* (Isaiah 60:2 NKJV).

You must realize that we are in the last days and in a time of deep darkness. That darkness is not just manifesting itself in communities, government, education, or through entertainment, it is also being transmitted through the medium of news broadcasts. Imbibing all of this darkness before going to bed can cause us to have nightmares or make our brains review the things that we watched earlier in the news as we sleep. These things will interfere with the genuine encounters that the Holy Spirit desires to give you.

ALWAYS BE READY TO RECORD
YOUR DREAMS

Always be prepared to record your dreams. I actually keep my iPad and my phone by my bedside. I keep my dreams in my note section on my iPad. The best time to record your dream is right after you awake from the dream because the details are fresh in your mind.

Keep in mind that a dream may not always come at an ideal time when you feel like you have been fully rested or when you are ready to start your day. A secret to receiving more revelation through dreams is properly valuing and recording the dreams that God has given you. If the Lord gives you a dream at three o'clock in the morning that causes you to wake up and your alarm is not set to go off until seven o'clock, don't roll over and go back to sleep. Some people forget the important details because they think they will remember them later. It is important to respond correctly to the dreams you receive so they occur more often.

How does the Lord want you to respond? Does He want you to stay awake and intercede for someone? Does He want you to write a few notes about the dream to refresh your memory later? Does He want you to take copious notes and write every detail? Whatever the case, you must be prepared to record the dream and respond to the Lord.

SPEND TIME MEDITATING ON YOUR DREAMS

Meditating on your dreams helps you establish a personal culture of thanksgiving for the wonderful encounters that God has given to you. Pondering our dreams helps to build our faith. I often go back to the dreams that I have recorded several years earlier because they are sources of encouragement to me.

Perhaps you are standing on the Word of God for some area of healing in your body and you had a dream that you were healed of that particular ailment two years ago. Keep focusing on that healing dream. God gave you the dream to encourage you so you can war against the enemy who may be telling you that you will not be healed.

Another reason for meditating on your dream is that the Lord may also be trying to increase your understanding of the dream. This has happened to me many times. As we continue to reflect on our dreams, we start to become more skilled in dream interpretation by studying the symbols in our dreams.

Last, as you spend more time reflecting on your dreams, you are showing God that you value the revelation He is sending you. Meditating on your dreams sends a message to Heaven that you are thankful and are ready for more. In essence, if you value what God is revealing to you, He will give you more dreams.

DREAMS MAY DECREASE DURING A TEST OR TRIAL

As a former high school teacher and seminary professor, I have given many exams and quizzes over the years. I have always tried to prepare my students thoroughly so they would be successful on the test. On the day of the actual exam, however, I stop instructing them because they must rely on their own preparation beforehand in order for them to do well on the test.

Similar to a teacher during an exam, God is quieter during a test. This is also true when it comes to dreams. During times of intense testing, dreams tend to decrease. So, during these times you must go back to what the Lord revealed in His Word, through personal prophecy, and through your dreams to encourage yourself in the midst of the trial.

NEVER BE SATISFIED WITH THE GIFT ALONE, YOU MUST DEVELOP IT

I have often reminded my son, who has a natural gifting for playing baseball, that he must keep working to improve himself. Ever since he was a toddler, I would pitch to him and he was able to hit most of the balls, particularly the fast ones. He was blessed with great hand-eye coordination. I had to communicate to him that natural giftedness would only take him so far in reaching his goals for baseball. He needed to develop his gift by working hard and studying all aspects of the game of baseball.

The same is true as it relates to being gifted to see in the spirit. We must never be content with having a spiritual gift. We need to mature in the gift by studying and gaining as much knowledge as we possibly can. As someone once said, "The more you know, the more you know that there is more to know." Be sure to read books that address dreams, visions, and the seer realm, which will increase your hunger for the things of God.

And finally, be sure to dwell in the secret place with your heavenly Father. Just enjoy spending time with Him and read His Word. This time spent with Him will keep you grounded so you don't become flaky, always seeking the spectacular. Remember to seek first the Kingdom of God and everything else, including dreams, will be added to you (see Matthew 6:33).

APPENDIX C

ACTIVATION PRAYER

I am a strong believer in impartation. We see examples from Scripture that spiritual gifts and anointing can be transferred from one person to another. The relationship between Paul and Timothy is a great example of the power of transference and activation.

> *Do not neglect the gift that is in you, which was given to you by prophecy with the laying on of the hands of the eldership. Meditate on these things; give yourself entirely to them, that your progress may be evident to all* (1 Timothy 4:14-15 NKJV).
>
> *Therefore I remind you to stir up the gift of God which is in you through the laying on of my hands* (2 Timothy 1:6 NKJV).

Paul also expressed his earnest desire to impart spiritual gifts to the believers in Rome so all could be mutually encouraged and strengthened in their faith (Romans 1:11-12). It is also my desire to be encouraged as I hear about the wonderful testimonies of you dreaming more, interpreting your own dreams, and being able to interpret the dreams of others after reading this book.

Although I am not able to physically lay hands on you right now, we serve the God who does miracles—and there is no distance too far in prayer. Even when the Lord Jesus walked the earth we observe from Scripture an interesting example of cross-pollination occurring with a man who was not part of the twelve disciples.

> John spoke up and said, "Teacher, we noticed someone was using your name to cast out demons, so we tried to stop him because he wasn't one of our group."
> "Don't stop him!" Jesus replied. "For the one who does miracles in the power of my name proves he is not my enemy. And whoever is not against us is for us" (Mark 9:38-40 TPT).

Dear reader, I offer the following prayer sincerely and humbly as a parting gift for you. I pray that the Lord will bless you and keep you—day and night.

ACTIVATION PRAYER

Father, I pray for this reader right now in the precious name of Jesus. I pray according to Ephesians 1:17-21 that the God of our Lord Jesus Christ, the Father of glory, may give to this child of Yours the spirit of wisdom and revelation in the knowledge of You, that the eyes of his or her understanding be enlightened to know the hope of Your calling.

I pray that this friend will know the riches of the glory of Your inheritance in the saints, and the exceeding greatness of Your power toward all who believe, according to the working of Your mighty power worked in Christ when You raised Him from the dead and seated Him at Your right hand in the heavenly places, far above all principality and power and might and dominion, and every name that is named, not only in this age but also in that which is to come.

It is also my prayer, Lord, that You will give this dear friend who has read this book the ability to recall their dreams with clarity and that You would activate this friend right now to see in the spirit realm and have supernatural dream encounters that draw You closer! Amen.

ABOUT
DR. CHARLES R. FOX

Dr. Charles R. Fox and his wife, April, are cofounders of Victory Breakthrough Ministries. He is the author of *Preparing for the Great Outpouring: Is Your Heart Ready for a Move of God?* and co-author of the book *William J. Seymour: Pioneer of the Azusa Street Revival.*

Charles is a seer and gifted communicator with a passion for revival. He also loves to equip people in the area of understanding and interpreting their spiritual dreams.

He and his wife reside in Bowie, Maryland.